NATIVES OF NORTHERN INDIA

NĀGA WARRIORS, ASSAM (p. 37)

The Native Races of the British Empire

NATIVES
OF
NORTHERN INDIA

BY

W. CROOKE, B.A.

OF THE BENGAL CIVIL SERVICE (RETIRED)

WITH THIRTY-TWO ILLUSTRATIONS

NIYOGI
BOOKS

Archives in historial reprints is a collaborative publishing effort between the NATIONAL ARCHIVES OF INDIA and NIYOGI BOOKS

Published by

NIYOGI BOOKS

D-78, Okhla Industrial Area, Phase-I
New Delhi-110 020, India
Tel: 91-11-26816301, 49327000
Fax: 91-11-26810483, 26813830
email: niyogibooks@gmail.com
www.niyogibooks.com

ISBN: 978-93-81523-44-5
Year of Publication: 2012

Printed at: Niyogi Offset Pvt. Ltd., New Delhi, India

EDITOR'S PREFACE

INTEREST in the subject races of the British Empire should be especially keen in the Mother Country, where there are few families but send into our dependencies some member, be it as Government official, soldier, or colonist. Anthropological text-books are at once too technical and too bulky to attract the ordinary reader, who wishes for no more than a sketch of habits and customs, accurate but readable, in which matter too abstruse, or otherwise unsuitable for general consumption, is omitted. The present series is intended to supply in handy and readable form the needs of those who wish to learn something of the life of the uncivilised races of our Empire; it will serve the purpose equally of those who remain at home and of those who fare forth into the world and come into personal contact with peoples in the lower stages of culture.

Unless otherwise stated the contributors to the series will be anthropologists who have personal knowledge of the tribes of whom they write; references to authorities will be dispensed with, as unnecessary for the general reader; but for those who desire to follow up the subject a bibliography will be found at the end of each volume.

The present series may perhaps do more than

merely spread a knowledge of the dark-skinned races beneath the British flag. Germany awoke years ago to the importance of the study of native races from a political and commercial, no less than from a scientific point of view. In twenty-five years the Berlin Museum has accumulated ethnographical collections more than ten times as large as those of the British Museum, and the work of collection goes on incessantly. England, with the greatest colonial empire which the world has ever seen, lags far behind. Money will perhaps be forthcoming in England for work in anthropology when savage life and savage culture has disappeared for ever from the earth before the onward march of so-called civilisation. If, one hundred years hence, English anthropologists have to go to Germany to study the remains of those who were once our subject races, we shall owe this humiliation to the supineness of England at the end of the nineteenth and beginning of the twentieth century. The past, once lost, can never be recovered; we have before us, in the subject races of our Empire, a living memorial of the past, and if England does her duty, she will lose no time in organising an Imperial Bureau of Ethnology, and thus enable English anthropologists to hold up their heads before their more fortunate German and American brethren.

NORTHCOTE W. THOMAS.

LONDON, *November* 22, 1906.

AUTHOR'S PREFACE

In this book, within a very limited space, an attempt has been made to describe the environment, race types, social and industrial life, and religious beliefs of the people of Northern India. I trust that it has been made clear that the area and population of this region are so great that in dealing with its inhabitants it has been necessary to avoid general statements as far as possible. The Punjabi stands to the Bengali much in the same relation as Scotsmen to Italians; they differ one from the other in race, character, language, and social institutions.

The scheme of the series does not allow of foot-notes with references to authorities. A bibliography of the books I have found most useful has been added. I desire to express my special indebtedness to the reports of the Census of 1901, conducted under the superintendence of Mr. Risley. While I cannot accept his conclusions on the race origins in their entirety, I fully recognise that his report marks a decided advance in the study of Indian ethnology, and the provincial reports, particularly those of Messrs. Gait and Rose, supply much valuable information.

For the photographs I am indebted to Mrs. G. M. Currie, Miss G. M. Godden, Messrs. G. R. Dampier, H. A. Rose, and Rev. A. Logsdail.

W. CROOKE.

CONTENTS

PAGE

EDITOR'S PREFACE, ... v

AUTHOR'S PREFACE, ... vii

CHAPTER I

DESCRIPTIVE

The country, its hills, rivers, plains. Brief historical sketch. Administrative divisions. The rivers, mountains, and hills. The deltas: the valleys: the plains: the desert. The influence of their environment upon the people, . . . 1

CHAPTER II

THE ETHNICAL ELEMENTS

Prehistoric races. The Ages of Stone and Copper. Three distinct physical types—the Indo-Aryan, the Dravidian, and the Mongoloid. The origin of the Dravidians. The Kolarian or Munda and the Dravidian branches. The Mongolians: the course of their migrations. The origin of the Bengali. The Aryan migration. The absence of Dravidians in the Punjab. The question of Baluchistan. The mixed races, . . . 16

CHAPTER III

THE TRIBES OF THE NORTHERN HILLS

The tribe. The Mongoloid tribe. The Nāgas, Angāmis: their villages: tribal structure. The Aos. The Semas. Head-hunting. The Bachelors' Hall. The Genna taboo. Nāga culture—arms, tartans, clothing. The Bhotiyas: Kashmiris: Dards: Baltis: Ladakhis: Pahāris: Dogras: Champas: Rajputs: Western Nāgas: Khasas: Gurkhas: Newārs: Afghāns: Pathāns: Baloch: Kāfirs, ... 36

CHAPTER IV

THE TRIBES OF THE SOUTHERN HILLS

PAGE

Kolis: Bhīls: Gonds. Status of the hill tribes. Conversion to Hinduism. Oraons: Kols: Mundas: Paharias: Santāls, 63

CHAPTER V

THE CASTES OF THE PLAINS

Caste: its conditions and origin. The tribal castes. The Rajput and Jat. The occupational castes. The Brahman. The Dom, ... 85

CHAPTER VI

THE AGRICULTURAL, COMMERCIAL, AND INDUSTRIAL CASTES OF THE PLAINS

Bhāts and Chārans. Bhuinhārs and Tagas. Khatris. Kayasths. Banyas. Halwāis. Rules of eating and drinking. Gūjars. Ahīrs. Kurmis. Mālis. Banjāras. Bhars. Thārus. Rājis. Kalwārs. Telis. Kols. Dhānuks. Dosādhs. Koris. Pāsis. Dhobis. Khatīks. Gipsy tribes — Gulgulias. Bhangis: Chamārs: Fakīrs, ... 106

CHAPTER VII

THE VILLAGE AND ITS INDUSTRIES: THE CRIMINAL AND VAGRANT TRIBES

The village craftsmen. Agriculture. Changes of occupation. The Jeweller. Other workers in metals. Carpenters: blacksmiths: potters: weavers: dyers: tailors: washermen. Vagrant, criminal, Gipsy tribes. Ods: Chāngars: Bāwarias: Aheris: Sānsis: Meos: Nats: Kanjars. Survival and decay of village industries, ... 126

CHAPTER VIII

HOME LIFE: THE OCCUPATIONS OF WOMEN

PAGE

The house. A Punjab village described. The cattle. The rest-house. The well and tank. The circles of soil. The year's farming work. The relaxation of the peasant. The work of women—preparation of food. The forest woman and her occupations. The silk industry. The work of the Gipsy woman. The wife of the artisan—spinning dyeing. Woman as a beast of burden. The care of cattle. Irrigation. Rice-planting. Husking and grinding grain. Cooking, . . . 150

CHAPTER IX

CHILD LIFE: GAMES AND AMUSEMENTS

Mystery of Indian child life. Isolation of children from Europeans. Lack of reverence. Sedateness, ease of manner. Etiquette. Conventions regarding children. Marriage arrangements. Pampering of children. Occupation of peasant children. Knowledge of Nature. Imaginativeness. Training of girls. Infant marriage, its origin and results. The mother-in-law. Training of boys. Amusements. Dancing. Persistence of habit. Tip-cat. Prisoners' Base. Leap-frog. Blind-man's Buff. Feats of strength and skill. Gulli Danda. Girls' games. Dolls. Mimic marriages. Floating away ill-luck, ... 173

CHAPTER X

THE BIRTH RITES

The theory of Taboo. Hindu ceremonies. Taboos of mother and child. The birth rite. The rite of the sixth day. Protection of mother and child. The naming rite. The initiation. The doctrine of metempsychosis. Mohammedan ceremonies. Rules enforced during eclipses. Precautions to avoid the Evil Eye. The naming rite. The circumcision, ... 194

CHAPTER XI

THE MARRIAGE RITES

PAGE

The prohibited degrees. The horoscope. The match-maker. Survivals of primitive forms of marriage. Marriage by purchase. Widow marriage. The marriage ritual among the forest tribes: among Brahmans, artisans and traders: among Mohammedans, ... 206

CHAPTER XII

DEATH RITES

Various modes of disposal of the dead. Burial and cremation. Exposure to wild beasts. Platform burial. Burial in its rudest form. Crouched burial. Niche burial. Burial of those under taboo. The Srāddha. Rites of the Mohammedans, ... 215

CHAPTER XIII

POPULAR RELIGION AND BELIEFS

Hinduism and Islām. Animism. The powers of Nature: Sun, Moon, Planets, Eclipses. Rivers and springs. Mountains. Spirits of the forest. Tree-worship. The jungle Mothers. Mother Earth: her marriage. The malignant Mothers. The village gods: their shrines. Malignant spirits: the Rākshasa, the Deo, the Daitya, the Bhūt. Animal-worship: Tigers, Snakes. Totemism. Progress of Animism into Hinduism, ... 223

CHAPTER XIV

MAGIC, SHAMANISM, WITCHCRAFT

Magic: its origin: its relation to Religion. Magic, White and Black. Imitative Magic. Magic by images. Rain-making. Nudity. Hair loosed. Contagious Magic. Identification of the magician. Magical spells. Black Magic. Controlling a demon. The charmed circle. Shamanism. Devil-dancing. Exorcism of disease. The village witch, ... 246

BIBLIOGRAPHY, ... 263

INDEX, ... 266

LIST OF PLATES

PLATE

1. Nāga warriors, Assam, ... *Frontispiece*
2. Rajput chief, United Provinces, . . . *facing page* 1
3. Hindu merchant, Western India, . . . ,, 16
4. Raja of Rampur, with attendants, Punjab hills, . ,, 32
5. Hindu girl in the Plains, ... ,, 48
6. Women in the Plains, showing dress and jewellery, . ,, 58
7. Panka, Dravidian weaver, southern hills, . . ,, 63
8. Baiswārs, Dravidian cultivators, southern hills, . ,, 68
9. Mānjhi cultivators, southern hills, with sacred drum, ,, 76
10. Bhotiyas of Kumaun, northern hills, ... ,, 90
11. Blacksmiths, Chota Nagpur, ... ,, 97
12. Brick-making, ... ,, 100
13. A potter at work, ... ,, 106
14. A naked Hindu Fakīr, Hardwar, . . . ,, 118
15. A Hindu Fakīr lying on a bed of nails, . . ,, 128
16. A Mohammedan Fakīr, ... ,, 138
17. A Kalwār, or seller of spirits, . . . ,, 147
18. Weavers at work, ... ,, 158
19. Carpenters at work, ... ,, 166

PLATE

20. A barber shaving a mourner, . . . *facing page* 173

21. Snake-charmers, ... „ 180

22. A troupe of Nautch-girls, ... „ 187

23. Her first lesson in spinning, ... „ 193

24. A peasant's hut, Bengal, ... „ 210

25. A Bhotiya village in the northern hills, Assam, . „ 218

26. Ploughing, ... „ 224

27. Harrowing and clod-crushing, . . . „ 230

28. A village scene, Bengal, ... „ 236

29. Women husking rice, Chota Nagpur, . . „ 240

30. Bathing in the Ganges, Hardwar, . . . „ 246

31. Pilgrims conveying Ganges water, . . . „ 252

32. Sacrificing a goat to the goddess Devi, . . „ 256

RAJPUT CHIEF, UNITED PROVINCES (p. 91)

NATIVES OF NORTHERN INDIA

CHAPTER I

DESCRIPTIVE

The country, its hills, rivers, plains. Brief historical sketch. Administrative divisions. The rivers, mountains, and hills. The deltas: the valleys: the plains: the desert. The influence of their environment upon the people.

NORTHERN INDIA consists mainly of a vast alluvial plain formed by three river systems, and separated from the plateau of Tibet by the Himālaya, 'the abode of snow,' the grandest mountain-range in the world. It is flanked on both sides by an ill-defined hill frontier —on the west the Sulaimān and Safed Koh, on the east the rough hill-country dividing it from Burma. On the south is a confused mass of hill and jungle stretching down to the rivers Nerbudda and Mahanadi, one draining into the Indian Ocean, the other into the Bay of Bengal.

The old Hindus called this plain the 'Middle Land,' and in later times the whole region which forms the subject of this sketch was called Hindostan, 'the abode of the Hindus,' in contrast to the Deccan or Southern India. But both these terms are used without precision, our school-books extending the name Hindostan to the whole Peninsula, while that of the Deccan is usually confined to the plateau between the rivers Nerbudda and Kistna.

To understand the origin of the races which occupy this country a brief survey of its history is needed.

When the Aryan tribes crossed the Himālaya they first settled in the south-west Punjab, and here the foundations of the Hindu religion and polity were laid. Buddhism had its origin further east in Behar, and here a great Buddhist Empire was founded and extended till, in the time of Asoka, it included all India proper from the 12th degree of latitude to the Himālayas, besides Nepal, Kashmir, part of the present kingdom of Kabul, with Sind and Baluchistan in the far west. This empire fell before successive assaults of the Kushān Scythians and Huns from Central Asia, and though the Hindu power was re-established under Harsha in the seventh century of our era, it decayed and was unable to resist the Mohammedan invasion, which, commencing in the tenth century, ended in the establishment of the Moghul Empire in the sixteenth. When the supply of fresh recruits from Central Asia ceased, the Moghul power became weakened, and, after the battle of Plassey in 1757, the British gradually succeeded to their inheritance.

For purposes of administration this region is at present divided into eight provinces or administrations. To the east lie Bengal and Assam, which have recently been formed into two provinces—Bengal and Eastern Bengal. West of these are the United Provinces of

Agra and Oudh, in the Gangetic valley; in that of the Indus the Punjab, from which the north-western frontier provinces were recently divided; and the agencies of Rajputana and Central India, including a number of independent, or quasi-independent, native states. To the south it includes parts of the Presidency of Bombay and the Central Provinces. It must, however, be remembered that these divisions are not marked by geographical or ethnical boundaries. They represent the gradual stages in the absorption of the native powers to whom the British succeeded, and their boundaries have been repeatedly changed to suit the convenience of their rulers.

Northern India, as thus defined, includes an area of about one million square miles—about one-third of the extent of the United States, rather less than double that of France, Italy, and the German Empire combined. Its population, one hundred and ninety-five millions, is half as great again as that of these three European states.

The chief factors in the environment of the people are threefold: the river system, the mountain and hill ranges, the climate and rainfall.

To begin with the rivers—three are of primary importance: the Indus and the Brahmaputra rising beyond the southern scarp of the Himālayas, the Ganges draining their lower slopes. The system of the Indus and its tributaries forms the alluvial plain of the Punjab and Sind; that of the Ganges waters the United Provinces and Bengal; that of the Brahmaputra enters India at the eastern extremity of the Himālayas and waters Assam and Eastern Bengal. These three rivers are snow-fed, and two of them, the Indus and the Ganges, furnish a constant supply of water to a great system of irrigation canals.

Next come the mountain and hill ranges. The Himālayas may be roughly divided into a higher and a lower range; but it is more accurate to call them a region rather than a mountain system. They stretch, a tangled mass of peaks and valleys, some fifteen hundred miles along the northern frontier. From lower heights on which the sanatoria, Simla, Dalhousie, Mussoorie, Naini Tal, and Darjiling are situated, the plains in the hot season appear to be covered with a reeking dust-haze. On the advance of the monsoon, masses of cloud strike the lower summits and dissolve into torrential rains. Behind this inferior range is a series of gigantic peaks still untrodden by the feet of man. Of these, Mount Everest, twenty-nine thousand feet high, is the highest measured mountain in the world.

The varying conditions of Himālayan orography in the west and east have profoundly affected the ethnology of those regions. To the west, fertile open valleys, such as those of Kashmir, Kulu, and Dehra Dun, provide easy routes into the northern hinterland. To the east, the malarious Terai bars communication between mountain and plain, and intercourse is still further restricted by the jealous native government of the Nepal valley and the barbarous tribes which occupy the lower hills flanking the valley of Assam. This northern mountain barrier is in most parts inaccessible to man throughout the eastern portion. In modern times it has been crossed by Chinese armies which have seriously threatened the Nepal valley, and by our forces which recently occupied Lhassa. But it nowhere yields a passage to large armies, and invasion of India through this region is practically impossible. Through the eastern gap, where the Brahmaputra forces its way through the Himālayas, it is probable that the Tibeto-Burman races entered India.

On the north-western frontier the case is different. Invaders from the north or north-west direction have repeatedly found their way down the courses of the Indus or Kabul rivers, after which no physical obstacle prevented their advance into the valley of the Ganges or even into Southern India through passes in the Vindhyan range. The northern part of this frontier, that occupied by Pathān tribes, is so difficult that its occupation by a disciplined army is practically impossible. Here and there it is pierced by passes which are the historical routes between Central Asia or Afghanistan and the Indian Plains. Such are to the north the Khyber and the Kurram, which open the way to Kabul; the less known Tochi, which probably gives access to Ghazni; and further south again the Gomal, which is used by the Ghilzai merchants of Southern Afghanistan. The difficulty of the Pathān problem depends on the fact that their hinterland is in Afghān keeping, and whenever they are involved in trouble with the Indian Government they not only have in their rear a safe sanctuary for their families and flocks, but they are certain to receive the sympathy and support of their kinsmen who are subject to the Amir. Their country is poor and unproductive, and they stand to the tribes in British territory very much in the same relation as that of Highlanders to Lowlanders before 1745.

The problems of administration in Baluchistan further south are much simpler, because the topographical conditions are much more favourable to the British overlords. This province, the creation of Sir R. Sandeman, has been opened to the world only within the last quarter of a century. While we have been unable to isolate the Pathān tribes of the north, in Baluchistan we hold positions in the rear of the most troublesome clans. As a result of this, brigandage has now practically ceased, because the hillmen find the game too dangerous.

Baluchistan is a region of varied character and fertility. Taking it as a whole, it exhibits a succession of rugged mountains, arid deserts, and stony plains with patches of cultivation wherever water is available, and occasional wooded hills, whose greenery affords a welcome relief to the eye wearied by the glare of the sun-baked rocks and gravel-strewn valleys. North Baluchistan, where the winter cold is intense, approximates in character to Afghanistan, and like it is occupied by Pathān tribes. The southern part is a country of excessive heat, and though little cultivated at present, the remains of irrigation-works show that it must at one time have been exceedingly fertile. 'O

God! When Thou hadst created Sibi and Dadhar, what object was there in conceiving hell?' says the native proverb.

Passing from the physical conditions of the northern frontiers, it remains to consider the southern boundary which separates Hindostan, as we have already defined it, from the Deccan or the southern portion of the Peninsula. This barrier consists of a tangled mass of hills and valleys which form, as it were, the backbone of the Peninsula, stretching from the Indian Ocean on the west almost as far as the Bay of Bengal on the east. These hill ranges cannot be grouped into a single well-defined system. On the west are the Aravallis, which divide that part of Northern India exposed to the monsoon rainfall from the arid deserts of Baluchistan. Further east the Vindhyas form the northern wall of the Nerbudda valley, and melt as they advance into the highlands of the Central Provinces. Further east again in the United Provinces and Bengal they are known as the Kaimūr and Rajmahāl ranges. In some places, as in the west and central parts of the range, the valleys or hill passes furnish easy access to immigrants from the north. But to the east, Chota Nagpur and the Santāl Parganas form an admirable refuge for the jungle races. In the former is a central tableland guarded on all sides by precipitous jungle-clad hills, and pierced here and there by rugged paths which a handful of resolute men could hold against a host of invaders. This plateau is a well-wooded, undulating country, where the abundant forests supply all the needs of these primitive races, and where there is scope for that form of shifting cultivation which suits them best. In the Santāl Parganas, abutting on the Gangetic valley, is the remarkable valley enclosed by hills and known as the Dāman-i-Koh, 'the skirts of the mountain,' which is the home of that interesting people, the Santāls.

To the ethnologist and student of primitive beliefs the races occupying the mountain and hill tracts which skirt the plains furnish a fascinating subject for investigation. But it must be remembered that the vast majority of the people of Northern India occupy the plains, while those residing in the Himālayan country or in the hills and plateaux of the south are in numbers quite inconsiderable.

It is the plains or alluvial valleys and deltas which are really important. We may roughly divide them into the deltaic, the higher valley, and the desert regions.

To begin with the deltas:—on the east the Ganges and Brahmaputra, as they approach the sea, pour down masses of mud and silt which form islands and gradually become fit for the plough. Bākarganj is a typical example of such a country, consisting largely of swamps where the people live a semi-amphibious life. The Sunderbuns, again, are a labyrinth of morasses, broken up into islands by a network of water-courses. This is sometimes swept by a tidal wave which overwhelms the villages with their people, crops, and cattle. In these humid deltas, disease follows the subsidence of the floods; cholera and various dangerous kinds of fever become endemic.

Like the Brahmaputra and the Ganges, the Indus to the west is gradually extending its delta at the expense of the sea. But the heat is greater and the moisture less abundant, and there are no water-logged jungles and morasses like those of the Sunderbuns.

At the foot of the Himālayas the Terai presents features in some degree analogous to those of the deltas. The drainage from the lower hills becomes choked, and the heat and dampness develop a luxuriant vegetation, great reedy swamps or savannahs of grass, the home of wild beasts and abounding in malaria. This land is quite unfit for man, except where small colonies of Thārus or cognate tribes make clearings during the healthier months of the year, gradually fell the jungle, and finally leave the farms to be occupied by the castes skilled in agriculture and the rearing of cattle who succeed them.

As we leave these pestilential parts of the country we meet the higher plains. In the middle reaches of the rivers, as in Bengal proper, the depressing and unhealthy nature of the climate shows its effects in the physique of the people. The Bengali and his cousin from Assam may be easily identified by their lanky stature, ill-developed muscular system, and want of robustness. With them, as with the Sindi of the Indus valley, the intellectual have grown at the expense of the physical qualities, and though they flourish in the present reign of peace, they would in troubled times fall easy victims to the stronger races of the upper plains and hills. The amount of rainfall is here the dominating factor. Where this is greatest, as in Bengal and Assam, rice is the chief crop, and supports a larger population than in the drier tracts. In the United Provinces and the Punjab the rainfall is less copious and the crops require artificial irrigation. In Baluchistan, the area of minimum rainfall, only nine inches per annum, there are eleven persons per square mile. The Bengal delta receives eighty inches of rain and supports 552 persons on a similar area.

One of the finest tracts in the Gangetic valley is the Doāb or Mesopotamia, between the rivers Ganges and Jumna. This, with Oudh and Rohilkhand to the north, forms a tract of marvellous fertility, responding generously to the labours of one of the finest peasant peoples. The country is watered from springs and canals, and the character of the husbandry differs widely from that of Bengal. The rice of the delta is here replaced by the maize, millets, and pulses, which form the food of the people, while the farmer pays his rent and derives his profits from wheat and barley, sugar, cotton, or opium. Irrigation, however, has dangers of its own, particularly where it is not accompanied by drainage. The subsoil becomes saturated, and the fierce heat attracts to the surface noxious salts which have rendered large areas unfertile. The productiveness of the soil, again, causes congestion of the people. In portions of North Behar there are as many as a thousand souls per square mile. Hence the castes which live by unskilled labour are in a wretched condition—ill-fed, ill-housed, ill-clothed, with no resources to withstand a failure of the rains and the scarcity, more or less severe, which attends such a calamity. The smaller tenants, rack-rented, obliged to borrow their food and seed grain, are in little better condition.

This great plain, uninteresting and monotonous as it may appear to the casual observer, is undoubtedly impressive. A traveller may march from Patna to Delhi, five hundred miles as the crow flies, without seeing a single eminence, except some ancient mound formed by the débris of the countless generations who have occupied the site. Mile after mile there is nothing which meets the eye but a closely cultivated country, each village shaded by its little grove, and here and there a patch of barren commonage grazed by the starveling cattle which work the well and provide milk. In the rainy season it is little more than a vast swamp diversified by patches of cultivation. But in the cold weather which follows, fields of wheat and barley stretch to the horizon, a sheet of verdure at Christmas time, yellow to harvest in March and April. Then comes the time of heat, when the air is full of a coppery dust-haze, varied by clouds of driving sand. All nature becomes torpid for a time, wakening to life again with the first breath of the rains.

Between the valleys of the Ganges and the Indus lies the agricultural danger-zone at the point where the two streams of the monsoon current, one moving up from the Bay of Bengal, the other from the Indian Ocean, converge. Ajmir, on the fringe of the western desert, is often deprived of its normal share of rain, and the same is the case in Bundelkhand, the tract south of the river Jumna. This is one of the most depressed and famine-stricken parts of Northern India. More arid still is the true desert of Rajputana, the bed of a primæval ocean, consisting largely of ridges of sand, like the ripples on a seashore. The villages are seldom fixed, because their permanence depends on the water supply, which is always scanty and sometimes brackish. Even to the south, where there is a river system of some importance, the average fertility nowhere approaches that of the Indus or Ganges valleys. But the keen, austere air of the desert has strengthened and refined the character and physique of its people.

In short, there is perhaps no region in the world where the inhabitants live under more diverse conditions, and where they have been more directly influenced by their environment, than in Northern India. Some races, like the Bhotiyas of Kumaun, and others of the Tibetan fringe, live in a land of perpetual snow, while in the Bengal delta the temperature hardly ever falls below 52 F. in the coldest season. There are districts, like those on the Assam borderland, where the rainfall amounts to some sixty feet in the year; in others, like Baluchistan and the desert of Rajputana, where it is scanty and precarious. In mode of life and general culture there are the most startling differences. Education flourishes in the deltas and in the larger cities, while, generally speaking, the rural classes in the plains are steeped in ignorance and superstition. Some frontier tribes of Assam and in the southern hill ranges are still in the savage stage—in Orissa, the Juāngs, for instance, having only quite recently abandoned the use of leaf garments. The highly developed system of farming in the Punjab and the United Provinces may be contrasted with the periodical felling and burning of the forest by the wilder hill races. The jungle-folk and the people of the plains display similar differences in their artistic skill and handicrafts. Some, like the Baloch, have few permanent settlements, moving their households in search of water and pasture for their flocks and herds. The nomad Doms of the plains have no habitation of any kind, sheltering themselves during rain under cattle-sheds and the eaves of houses. Others, like the Sānsiyas, erect crazy shelters of mats or cloth. The Bengali peasant lives under a flimsy hut roofed with bamboos and leaves, while in the Punjab and Rajputana the house has walls of brick or consolidated clay. In religion we need only compare the Brahman philosopher of Benares with the Animist dweller in the jungle.

Differences like these extend to the social relations of all classes. Thus in the Himālayan districts the local politics depend upon the configuration of the country. The area of cultivatable land in the narrow valleys is small, and it has been necessary to utilise every scrap of fertile soil on the slopes by means of terrace cultivation. The farms are therefore scattered; no large villages with resources for self-defence can be founded, and the natural tendency is towards the creation of petty kingdoms, isolated from one another by physical obstacles, and incapable of cohesion to resist a common enemy. So in the plains some tribes, like the Gūjars, prefer to plant their villages on the crest of the higher alluvium, where they carry on a certain amount of tillage in a lazy and improvident way, and feed the herds of buffaloes on which their livelihood mainly depends, in the rank swamps along the river side. Mr. Baden-Powell remarks that in the Punjab 'the location of Mohammedan villages usually follows the river lowlands, where cultivation is less troublesome, and the crop more secure, though the climate is less healthy. The Jats and hardier agricultural races, on the other hand, follow the higher lands, where the soil is good, but the labour of raising a full crop more considerable; the climate, however, is drier and much healthier.' This difference of climate is illustrated by a comparison of the physique of these two castes. Differences of crops and food are equally apparent throughout the whole country.

When we come, lastly, to consider the imaginative and intellectual faculties, the influence of environment is no less important. The great majority of the population inhabits the plains, and here they are so absorbed in the toil of farming, or engrossed in petty trade, that they are blind to the beauty which at certain seasons characterises the landscape. In this flat monotonous country there is little temptation to travel, because one village with its tank, grove, and temple is the counterpart of another. Nature here displays herself in her more ruthless moods—torrential rains at one season, scorching heat in another, hailstorms or earthquakes, outbreaks of disease the dangers of which are intensified by the neglect of sanitary precautions habitual to the people. Congestion of population in many parts involves a struggle for bare existence which begins with childhood and ends only with the grave. This condition of things encourages a pessimistic mode of belief, an apathetic submission to the spirits, mostly malignant, which are believed to control human life. A powerful priesthood and the bondage of caste repress originality of thought and freedom of action. Hence comes the habitual melancholy of the people of the plains which strikes every observer. They seem to talk of little but food and bargaining, of the petty squabbles and jealousies of the hamlet. To save or borrow a little money for a wedding or a funeral is their main object in life. On the other hand, it is only in the hilly tracts that we meet really cheery, light-hearted people like the Oraons and Mundas of Chota Nagpur and the Gurkhas of Nepal.

So far we have been considering the physical and climatic environment, and suggesting some of the ways in which it affects the people. But besides the differences thus created, there are distinctions of race, and the population represents the fusion of many strains of blood. This will form the subject of the next chapter.

CHAPTER II

THE ETHNICAL ELEMENTS

Prehistoric races. The Ages of Stone and Copper. Three distinct physical types—the Indo-Aryan, the Dravidian, and the Mongoloid. The origin of the Dravidians. The Kolarian or Munda and the Dravidian branches. The Mongolians : the course of their migrations. The origin of the Bengali. The Aryan migration. The absence of Dravidians in the Punjab. The question of Baluchistan. The mixed races.

WE considered in the last chapter the physical environment and its influence upon the people. It now becomes necessary to deal with the elements, prehistoric and historic, out of which they have been formed.

Our knowledge of the prehistoric races is slight, because the sepulchral remains and rude stone monuments which abound on the plateaux of Southern India are scanty in the north. We can trace, as the archæologists of Europe have done, a palæolithic period characterised by rude stone implements; the neolithic, with those of polished stone; and the age of copper. Stone implements of both periods have been found throughout the entire Peninsula, from Madras in the south, along the western coast as far as the valley of the Indus; all through the plateau of the Deccan with its girdle of hills; and far to the east in Burma.

Hindu Merchant, Western India (p. 111)

They have been discovered in Northern India at considerable depths in the alluvium, and beneath the sites of the oldest human settlements. They abound all along the backbone of the Peninsula, the Satpura, Vindhya, and Rajmahāl hills, and in some places what seem to be manufactories of these implements have been unearthed. Here, as in many other places, the ages of rough and polished stone overlap, and there is no evidence to fix the sequence of the races who may have used them.

Caves and rock-shelters have been discovered in the Vindhyan range, in which the jungle-folk are depicted pursuing the Gaur or great wild ox and the Sāmbhar stag with lances furnished with blades of stone. It is impossible to define the age of these rock drawings, which resemble those of the South African or Australian tribes. They are executed in hematite, a substance which under favourable circumstances may endure for a considerable time. But it must be noted that in this part of the country the greater fauna survived until Moghul times.

These people used these weapons in the modes familiar to students of primitive man—some as battle-axes or weapons of offence and defence, or for grubbing up wild roots, for which purpose they have now been replaced by the khanta or iron-shod spud employed by the women of the Korwa and allied tribes. Others may have been used to scoop out canoes or wooden vessels, the operation being facilitated by a preliminary charring with fire. Many were used as skin-scrapers, and the curious 'pygmy' flints may have

B

taken the place of needles or borers. The mystery which surrounds these weapons has caused the tribes of our day to regard them as sacred. They are frequently deposited on the shrines of the village gods; in fact, there is some reason to believe that many of them may have been made as offerings to the deities who preside over agriculture, the chase, and the rude industries of this semi-savage people.

There is no proof that the age of stone was followed by an age of bronze, the objects of that metal found being probably articles of luxury imported from abroad. But an age of copper is well marked by finds of implements of remarkable shapes in the Ganges valley. These, however, are questions for the archæologist rather than the ethnographer, because we possess no materials by which to establish connection between the tribes who used these primitive weapons and the present population.

Even the most unobservant visitor begins soon after his arrival in the country to discriminate a few of the more striking physical types. The evidence from physiognomy and other obvious characters has in recent years been supplemented by a considerable number of measurements, on which Mr. Risley and others have attempted to frame a race classification. The general conclusions which have been reached in this way are undoubtedly of considerable value. They coincide with the evidence from history and linguistics, so far as it has been collected. But when anthropometry claims to do more than distinguish the main types, and when its methods are applied to individual tribes or castes, it becomes obvious that the foundation is unable to bear the stately structure which has been reared upon it.

In the first place, we are not at present in possession of a complete series of skull measurements of the people of India, still less of its borderlands. Secondly, these measurements are confined to skull and nasal forms. Though these may be of primary value, it is rash to base the classification of such a complex organisation as the human frame on these organs alone. Skull and nose measurements, while valuable as a test of race types, seem to fail when applied to the mixed races and half-breeds which form the majority of the people. The race migrations are all prehistoric, and the amalgamation of the races has continued for ages among a people to whom moral restraints are irksome and unfamiliar. The existing castes are quite a modern creation, dating only from the later Buddhist age.

If we could bring together in a single group specimens of the leading races, it would be possible to select without difficulty at least three leading types.

The first is a man with a relatively long head; the nose aquiline, sometimes straight and finely moulded; the face is long and symmetrically narrow, with a well-developed forehead; the features are regular and the facial angle high—that is to say, he shows no signs of prognathism as it appears in the coarsely projecting lower jaw of the Negroid races. He is of tall stature, so tall, that a high-class Sikh regiment on parade compares favourably with one of our British Guard battalions. Among the higher members of this race the skin-colour is a light transparent brown, 'wheat-coloured,' as the people themselves describe it. The woman is tall and robust, with a fine independent carriage, her figure untrammelled by corset, her feet never tortured in fashionable shoes. If she be a member of a well-to-do family she is often secluded, and whenever she does venture abroad she conceals her face, not in the hideous mode adopted by the Mohammedan lady of rank, but with a veil which hangs coquettishly from her head. Her complexion is brunette, hardly darker than that of a Spaniard or Italian.

The best representatives of this type are found among the Brahmans of Kashmir, or the high-caste people of the Punjab, or the western desert. In intellect the Kashmiri Brahman is superior to the people of the northern plains. His only rival in cleverness is the Mahratta Brahman. As a stranger to Hindostan he is naturally suspected, and in a popular proverb he is ranked with the Afghān and Kamboh—a trio of rascals. But in spite of this, many men of his race have reached high positions in the public service and learned professions. The first native who gained a seat on the Bench of the Calcutta High Court was not a Bengali but a Kashmiri.

This type has been called by Mr. Risley the Indo-Aryan (Plate 6).

In sharp contrast to this fair people is the dark type, which has been styled the Dravidian—a term which is properly linguistic, originally applied to the languages of the south, but extended by modern Indian ethnologists to the races which speak these tongues. Mr. Risley, by an undue expansion of the term, applies the name to the mass of the population of Northern India—all, in fact, which is not the result of foreign immigration—Aryan, Scythian, or Mongoloid. The purest examples of this race are found among the degraded Karumbas and Irulas of the Nilgiri Hills. In the north they are represented by the Gonds, Oraons, Kols, Mānjhis, and Baiswārs of the Vindhyan range (Pls. 3, 17).

In stature they are below the mean; their complexion very dark, almost approaching black; the hair is long, worn in unkempt masses hanging down from the back of the head, and with a slight tendency to curl. The head is long, the nose very broad, sometimes depressed at the root, but not so as to make the face appear flat. Their appearance reminds us of Swift's description of the Yahoo, probably based on some Negroid type: 'the face of it was flat and broad, the nose depressed, the lips large, the mouth wide.' In general character they approach the Negritos, but they differ from them in form of skull, and though their skin is very dark, it never reaches the sooty blackness of the true Negrito, and the jaw though coarsely moulded is never prognathous as among the West African races. In person they are robust, muscular in shoulder and thigh, with lean fore-arm and lower leg.

Captain Forsyth describes the Gonds of the Central Provinces as intensely shy, stolid, but good-humoured and distrustful of foreigners. Some of the younger men and girls are comely, but the hard life of the jungle soon gives them a coarse, weather-beaten aspect. The Gond matrons of the inner hills are, he says, more like monkeys than human beings, the features strongly marked and coarse. 'The young girls occasionally possess such comeliness as attaches to general plumpness and a good-humoured expression of face; but when their short youth is over, all pass at once into a hideous age.' The women dress decently enough in a short petticoat tucked in between the legs so as to leave them naked to the thigh, and a mantle of cotton covering the upper part of the body, with a fold thrown over the head. Wherever the skin is exposed, it is tattooed in conventional designs, and like other savages they delight in wearing a profusion of coarse jewellery, the arms and legs being generally loaded with tiers of heavy rings, made of silver among the more wealthy, among the poorer of brass, iron, or coloured glass. The dress of the men is miserably scanty, a small loin-cloth generally representing the whole wardrobe.

Writing of the branch of the same race in the hill country of Bengal, Mr. Risley lays special stress on the form of the nose. 'It is hardly a paradox,' he remarks, 'to lay down as a law of the caste organisation of Eastern India, that a man's social status varies in inverse ratio to the width of his nose.' This distinction is at once apparent when we contrast the nose index of the Punjab Gūjar, a fairly typical Indo-Aryan (66·9), with that of the Malē of the Santāl Parganas, a true Dravidian (94·5). In stature the contrast between the two races is equally decided. These Malēs have a mean stature of 157·7 as compared with 174·8 in the Rajput of the western plains.

The third characteristic type easily recognisable in a representative crowd is the Mongoloid. This race in Tibet has a yellow complexion, narrow slant eyes, small nose, laterally prominent malar bones, black lank hair, and short stature. On the Indian side of the Himālayas the type differs to some extent where-ever they have come in contact with the natives of the plains, and it often happens that one branch has been exposed to foreign influence more than another. Thus the Lepchas of western Bhotan, Nepal, and Sikhim, as described by Colonel Dalton, are of fairly pure Mongoloid blood. The stature of the men is about five feet, the women bearing to them about the normal proportion. 'The face,' he says, 'is broad and flat, nose depressed, eye oblique, no beard, but a little moustache, complexion olive, and boys and girls in health have generally a ruddy tinge which adds greatly to their good looks. The total absence of beard, and the fashion of parting the hair along the crown of the head, gives to the males a somewhat effeminate appearance, and the robes of the sexes being somewhat alike, it is not always easy to distinguish them. They are proud of their hair and careful in its arrangement, the women wearing theirs behind braided in two tails tied with silken cords and tassels.' The Limbus, who are the chief cattle-merchants and butchers in Sikhim, are described by

Colonel Waddell as flatter in face and much more markedly Mongolian than the Lepchas, and this in spite of the fact that they have adopted the dress and external observances of the Hindus. In fact, the race is here rapidly becoming mixed. The difficulty of classifying these border tribes is illustrated in the case of the semi-aborigines of the Duārs in north Assam. Colonel Dalton, Mr. Risley and others, include them among 'the dark negro-like aborigines of India, the Dravidians'; while Colonel Waddell, an equally competent authority, calls them distinctly Mongoloid.

The most important physical peculiarity of these Mongoloid races is that they are distinctly broad-headed, in contrast with the Indo-Aryan and Dravidian types in which the skull is long.

We thus recognise three distinct physical types. But these remain distinct only on the very outskirts of Northern India—Aryans in the north and north-west Punjab, Dravidians in the secluded districts of the Central Provinces, Mongoloids in the hills fringing the valley of Assam. Everywhere else these types have become intermingled and confused, and the bulk of the population represents the mixture of one or more in varying proportions. Thus in the Central Provinces the basis is Dravidian, but they have been influenced by other strains of blood—Hindus or Aryans from the north, Mahrattas from the Deccan, Oriyas from Orissa. The present population thus represents the flotsam and jetsam collected from many streams of ethnical movement, and as a result of this there is a bewildering variety of language and dialect. We find examples of all the Aryan tongues spoken between Gujarat on the west and Bengal on the east, from the Himālayas on the north to the Deccan on the south. These languages have contributed to form many varieties of mongrel speech. In short, language is here no more permanent than race. While the Bhīls of the Central Provinces retain their original Dravidian tongue, in Rajputana many of them speak an impure form of Gujarati, an Aryan language.

We must now attempt to discuss very briefly the origin of these three typical race forms, and to trace their development on Indian soil.

It will be convenient to start with the Dravidians (an unsatisfactory term, but now too well established to be abandoned), who if not the original inhabitants of the Peninsula, are the oldest race the existence of which can be established with reasonable certainty. They are spoken of in the Vedic Hymns as Dasyus or Dasas, a term which has been interpreted to mean 'foes.' The poets call them 'noseless,' with reference to the broad nose and coarse nostril which they show to the present day. The ancient geographers told strange tales about them. We hear of people 'five or even three spans in height, some of whom want the nose, having only orifices above the mouth through which they breathe. They dwell near the sources of the Ganges, and subsist on the savour of roasted flesh, and the perfumes of fruit and flowers.' They carry apples with them that they may have something to smell when on a journey. Some have their feet turned backwards, like demons all the world over. Some are men 'with dog-shaped heads, armed with claws, clothed with skins, who speak not in the accents of human language, but only bark, and have fierce grinning jaws. They cover their body, which is all over hairy, with the soft down found on the leaves of trees.' The Vedic singers call them eaters of raw flesh, and godless; but they admit that they had forts and castles and possessed much wealth, and that the Aryans deigned to enter into matrimonial alliances with them.

Two main theories of the origin of this people occupy the field: one that they are allied to the Oceanic Negritos in whom are included the aborigines of Australia and Tasmania,—some authorities proposing to regard the Dravidians as a cross with a negroid race, and the alleged discovery of frizzly-haired Dravidians lends some support to this view;—the other, that they entered India from some region to the north or west.

In support of the first theory it has been suggested by Dr. Grierson that there is a resemblance between some Australian dialects and the Munda family of languages spoken by the Kols and other tribes of the Bengal hills. But Dr. Steinkonow holds that the resemblance is purely formal, and not due to any fundamental unity of the language. Another fact is adduced to support the connection of the Dravidians with the Negritos of the south, that the boomerang is used both in Australia and by certain Indian tribes like the Kallans of Madras. The boomerang seems to be only an aberrant form of the throwing-stick, a common savage weapon, and that form of it which makes a circuit and then returns to the person who hurled it may have been independently invented by more than one savage tribe. In further support of the Negrito hypothesis it has been argued that in prehistoric times a continent existed now submerged in the Indian Ocean, and that by this a route from Australia to India or *vice-versâ* may have been available.

The second hypothesis assumes that the Dravidians were divided into two branches: the Kolarians speaking Mundari, and the Dravidians proper, whose languages are of the family represented by the Tamil of Madras. The former are supposed to have entered India from the north-east, while the latter migrated from the direction of the Euphrates-Tigris valley. The two streams of foreigners converged in Central India. The pure Dravidians proved the stronger and thrust aside the Kolarians, after which they occupied the south of the Peninsula. The only substantial argument in favour of the hypothesis of the origin of this race from the north-west is found in the remarkable Brahui tribe in Baluchistan. It is quite certain that they speak a language closely allied to the speech of the Bengal hill races, and the puzzle is how this small body of people continues to use a Dravidian tongue. It seems clear that the Brahuis are either the rear-guard of a body of emigrants from the north-west, or the advance-guard of those migrating from the south. On the whole, the latter supposition seems the more probable, and from what we know of the ethnology and culture of the early people of Babylonia, it is very unlikely that the Dravidians should have emigrated from that region.

Further, it is now well established that in physique the so-called Kolarians are identical with the Dravidians of the south. It is true that they speak different tongues; but Dr. Grierson has recently proved that these languages belong to the same family. The Munda language of the Bengal hills is of a more archaic type than those of Madras, and the linguistic evidence leads to the conclusion that both races came from the south, and that they must have remained apart for a period sufficiently long to admit of the development of those peculiarities which differentiate the languages of the so-called Kolarian or Munda group from those of the other Dravidians.

In the present stage of our knowledge, then, all that can be advanced with certainty towards the solution of the Dravidian problem is that from very early times, long before the dawn of history, we find in the lower slopes and plateaux of the Nilgiri hills and in other parts of Southern India a swarthy, low-sized, long-headed, broad-nosed race in occupation of the country. Whether they were autochthones, or whether they succeeded, as some suppose, an earlier race, it is impossible to decide with any degree of confidence. In this part of the country they seem to have reached a fairly high stage of culture. They were probably the builders of the remarkable series of rude stone monuments which crown the hills in the Nilgiri range and the plateau of the Deccan. Excavations of their burial mounds prove that they had acquired considerable artistic skill. The urns in which they deposited the remains of their dead are plain but well-designed, and the clay figures representing men and animals which are found with the sepulchral urns, while exhibiting no very high level of ceramic art, are interesting, as they depict the arms, utensils, and dress of a race which has been long forgotten.

These southern Dravidians were a maritime people, and in their burial mounds are found bronze articles which were probably imported in the course of trade with Babylonia. These merchants, availing themselves of the monsoons, used at the beginning of the seventh, and perhaps up to the end of the eighth, century B.C., to sail from the south-west coast of India to ports at the mouth of the Euphrates. The trade terms, such as the names used in the time of Solomon for ivory, apes, and peacocks, are Tamil; in other words, they come from a Dravidian, not a Sanskrit tongue. It was these merchants, as Professor Rhys Davids believes, who brought to India the letters of the old Akkadian script, which became the prototype of all the alphabets used in India, Burma, Siam, and Ceylon.

It is perhaps reasonable to suppose that colonies of this race, forced to abandon their homes in Southern India, may have pushed their way northward into the central hill tract and thence to the plains beyond. Their first settlements may have been the highlands which they occupy to the present day. Such a land exactly met the needs of their system of husbandry, and it was they who undertook the gigantic task of clearing the northern plains, then probably covered with dense jungle. They were the first to appreciate the benefits of irrigation, and the shape of many of the more ancient tanks proves that they were constructed by them.

In this region we still find the Dravidian tribes acting as the pioneers of agriculture. 'Labour,' says Mr. Risley, 'is the birthright of the pure Dravidian. and as a coolie he is in great demand wherever we meet him. Whether hoeing tea in Assam, the Duārs, and Ceylon, cutting rice in the swamps of Eastern Bengal, or doing scavenger's work in the streets of Calcutta, Rangoon, and Singapore, he is recognisable by his black skin, his squat figure, and the negro-like proportions of his nose. In the upper strata of the vast social deposit which is here treated as Dravidian, these typical characteristics tend to thin out and disappear, but even among them traces of the original stock survive in varying degrees.'

The northern Dravidians have now fallen almost altogether under the Hindu yoke. Scholars have searched in vain for traces of Dravidian survivals in the Indo-Aryan tongues which form the vernacular speech. Those tribes which still speak their original tongue are replacing it by Aryan languages. It is only in Southern India that Tamil, Telugu, and allied Dravidian languages flourish, and have been gradually developed into a literary vehicle combining strength and that elasticity which adapts them to the needs of an advancing culture. In Northern India it is only the most isolated tribes which continue to speak their original language.

The social institutions of the Dravidians differ

widely from those of the Aryans. In India nothing more closely affects the people than the system under which the land is held, and the Dravidians worked out the problem in a way quite different from that of their conquerors. The village of Central and Southern India, says Mr. Baden-Powell, 'marked by the existence of an influential hereditary headman, and by the methods of allotting free lands as the special privilege of the village chief and the accountant, as well as to remunerate the hereditary staff of artisans and servants, is the direct descendant and surviving representative of the old Dravidian form of agricultural settlement.' But in the north its place has been taken by the village community, which is generally the result of a clan settlement of a tract of waste land or of a clearing made by Dravidians who were reduced to the position of serfs and menials. 'In short,' to quote the same writer, 'the quasi-feudal organisation of Rajputana, the old ideals of monarchy still traceable in the existing Hindu states, the Purānic religion, the law of the text-books, and the complete establishment of caste, these are all due to the Aryans settled beyond the Saraswati and the Jumna, in the Ganges Plain.

The second race element, the Mongoloid, is much less important. The original seats of this race lie north of the Himālayan range. It is only in the region of Bengal, Assam, and Burma that the strain has affected the present population to any considerable extent. In the Punjab and the United Provinces it is almost entirely absent. As an explanation of this fact

Mr. Risley supposes that at an early period the Aryan tribes occupying the western Himālayas through the fertile valleys, like those of Kashmir, checked the Mongolian inroad in that direction, while the effeminate races of the Brahmaputra and lower Ganges were unable to make any effective resistance. There may be some truth in this view, but it must be remembered that we are dealing with prehistoric race movements, and we have no real evidence to show why the Mongolian invasion was diverted eastward. All that we do know is that successive waves of these tribes passed down the valleys of the great eastern rivers—the Brahmaputra, Chindwin, and Irawaddy—and drove their predecessors, who seem to have been Dravidians, into the mountain fastnesses overlooking the valleys, and finally overwhelmed and absorbed them.

The chief interest in this Mongolian element rests on the fact that it accounts for the broad head of the Bengali, by which he is distinguished both from the Aryan and the Dravidian. The older school of ethnologists believed that the Bengali stood in the relation of cousinhood to the Englishman. This conclusion rested on philological considerations, Bengali and English being both of the Aryan family of languages, and thus to some extent allied in structure and vocabulary. Language, we now understand, is not a test of race, but it may explain tribal migrations. When we find a body of persons speaking a language or dialect which is not that of the locality in which they are found, we may reasonably conclude that at some time or other they must have lived in the area

No. 4

Raja of Rampur, with Attendants, Punjab Hills (p. 20)

where it was the prevailing speech. But this is a very different matter from concluding that the Bengali is allied to the Englishman because they both speak languages of the same family. As a matter of fact, the broad-headed Bengali is much less closely related to the Englishman than the Kashmiri or Punjabi.

This brings us to the Aryan, the last of the three great race types. The term, like Dravidian, is ambiguous. In one of his later essays Professor Max Müller thus emphatically protests: 'I have declared again and again that if I say Aryas, I mean neither blood nor bones, nor hair nor skull; I mean simply those who speak an Aryan language. The same applies to Hindus, Greeks, Romans, Germans, Celts, and Slaves. When I speak of them I commit myself to no anatomical characteristics. . . . To me an ethnologist who speaks of the Aryan race, Aryan blood, Aryan eyes and hair, is as great a sinner as a linguist who speaks of a dolichocephalic dictionary, or a brachycephalic grammar. It is worse than a Babylonian confusion of tongues—it is downright theft. We have made our own terminology for the classification of languages; let ethnologists make their own for the classification of skulls, and hair, and blood.' Hence we may be spared the investigation of the seats or physical characteristics of the original Aryans. With us it is merely a convenient term to express the white type of man, of whom the best specimens are to be found among some of the races of the Punjab.

All that we really know of this so-called Aryan race

is that they came into India from the north or west, and when literary evidence—that of the Vedic hymns—begins, we find them settled in the Holy Land of the Hindus in the south-western Punjab. Thence they gradually advanced down the river valleys to the east and south. The remarkable fact remains that while to the east and south we can recognise an Indo-Aryan race of overlords and a lower stratum of black menials, in the Punjab, from the Rajput and Brahman at the top, down to the scavenger at the bottom, the race type is uniform. That is to say, from the earliest times the valley of the Five Rivers must have been a land of white men. Here the Aryans did not intermarry with the dark daughters of Heth. If caste, as many authorities believe, was the result of the clash of a white with a black race, it could not have originated in this region.

Mr. Risley has devoted much ingenious speculation to explain this remarkable fact. Here it is possible only to state the general result of the discussion. If the race remained pure in the Punjab, it seems obvious that they must have been accompanied by their wives. It is assumed that a migration of this kind could not have been accomplished through the north-western passes, like the Khyber, which offer a difficult route for heavily laden caravans. It has, therefore, been suggested that they used the southern route through Baluchistan, which at that time, as appears from the ruins of canals and embankments which stud the country, must have been a fertile land where the advancing tribes could halt, refresh their animals, and prepare for a fresh movement onwards. Later, it is believed that the fertility of Baluchistan deteriorated, and this route became closed, with the result that the tribes which followed the first settlers were compelled to use the more northerly passes through which men alone could travel. They were thus compelled to ally themselves with the Dravidian tribes of the east and south.

The difficulty in this theory is to prove that the early fertility of Baluchistan was contemporaneous with a migration of which we have no historical evidence, and it seems to lose sight of the fact that even in our times the northern passes are used largely by caravans which include women and children. Such may have been the condition of things from the very earliest ages, and if we admit, as is probable, that the southward movement of the Aryan tribes extended over a long period of time, there is no difficulty in supposing that the Punjab, then presumably a land without inhabitants, may have been gradually colonised from Central Asia.

The general result is, then, that Northern India was peopled by three distinct strains—the white, the yellow, the black. These have now become so intermixed and confounded that it is impossible to say where one variety of man ends and another begins.

CHAPTER III

THE TRIBES OF THE NORTHERN HILLS

The tribe. The Mongoloid tribe. The Nāgas, Angāmis: their villages: tribal structure. The Aos. The Semas. Head-hunting. The Bachelors' Hall. The Genna taboo. Nāga culture—arms, tartans, clothing. The Bhotiyas: Kashmiris: Dards: Baltis: Ladakhis: Pahāris: Dogras: Champas: Rajputs: Western Nāgas: Khasas: Gurkhas: Newārs: Afghāns: Pathāns: Baloch: Kāfirs.

WHEN we examine the social organisation of the people of Northern India we find that some of them are divided into tribes, and some into castes. The tribe is a collection of families or groups of families bearing a common name; its members generally claim descent from a mythical or historical ancestor, and occasionally from an animal; but in some parts of the country the tribesmen are held together by the obligation to assist their brethren in blood feuds, rather than by the tradition of a common ancestry. They usually speak the same language, and occupy or profess to occupy a definite tract of country. A tribe is not necessarily endogamous, that is to say, it is not a general rule that a man of a particular tribe must marry a woman of that tribe, and cannot marry a woman of another tribe.

Putting aside the question of the origin of the tribe, it is sufficient to say that in order of time it probably precedes the caste. It is found in most vigour in the hill tracts which are the home of the most primitive races. The conditions of the hill-country are peculiarly favourable to the growth of these self-independent tribes. Each narrow valley with terrace cultivation on the adjoining slopes supports a small number of families, isolated from the outer world, and depending upon their own labour for all the necessaries and most of the luxuries of life. Few people in India enjoy a happier life than the residents of some of these valleys. In Kulu, for instance, the farmer grows his yearly stock of food from his own little croft, and his sheep and goats supply him with milk and materials for his clothing. Tobacco, his chief luxury, he also grows for himself, and he supplies his other wants by bartering his produce. In fact, the visitor complains that he is too prosperous because he objects to work as a porter and declines to furnish supplies at a reasonable price.

As a typical example of the most savage form of tribe we may select that of the Mongoloid races of Assam and its borderland. This hill-country is occupied by groups of tribes whose customs and institutions are of the most archaic type. Beginning from the west are Akas, Daflas, Miris, Abors, and Mishmis, of whom a moiety, partially civilised, live within British territory, and the residue, preserving a ruder form of culture, occupy the wild country which, nominally included in Tibet, is really independent.

To the east of the Assam valley the Nāgas form a compact group. They are by far the most interesting of the Mongoloid tribes, and we know much more about them than about the northern tribes, who are only partially within British influence. They number in all about 162,000 souls, and their country has been thoroughly explored by Colonel Woodthorpe, Messrs. Damant, Davis, and others. In some respects they are in a state of savagery only to be compared with that of the wildest races in the Indian Empire—the Was of Upper Burma, and the Jarwas of the Andaman Islands. Their fierce tribal feuds, their disregard of the sanctity of human life, their habit of raiding the settled villages on their borders in search of slaves or heads, illustrate the fiercer side of their character. On the other hand, they have attained considerable skill in agriculture and in the ruder arts of life.

The largest of the Nāga tribes and that of which we possess the most complete knowledge is the Angāmi. Their culture is so far superior to that of the other members of the group that, while the latter raise their crops by periodically felling and burning a patch of forest, the Angāmis grow their rice on terraces dug out from the hillsides with great skill and labour, and they water it by means of channels excavated for long distances along the contours. This art Mr. Davis supposes to have come from Manipur in the south, which the Angāmis believe to have been their original home. This improved style of farming seems to have been adopted because they have become accustomed to a diet of rice in place of the coarser grains which their wilder kinsfolk use. Rice-growing is impossible in the elevated country which they occupy without artificial irrigation, which cannot be provided when the holding is periodically abandoned in the old, thriftless fashion.

Their villages are designed to protect the inhabitants from the attacks of hostile tribes. Each is a stockaded fortress situated on an eminence, the houses being massed together without much attempt at arrangement, and the settlement guarded by an almost impenetrable fence of thorny shrubs and stinging nettles. Narrow sunken paths give entrance to the enclosure, the actual gateway being protected by a strong wooden door. At the present day this is seldom closed, an indication that British rule is gradually repressing intertribal warfare. The better dwellings follow the type of the long house common in Eastern Asia. The chief's palace, if it may be so called, is often 250 or 300 feet in length, and occupies the centre and highest position in the village. Much trouble is expended in the decoration of a house. The approaches to the village are planted with trees, beneath which are the receptacles which contain or cover the remains of their dead. This habit of burial close to the house produces among them an attachment to their village sites which is unusual among the hill tribes. Nothing short of the direst necessity will force them to abandon a place consecrated, as they believe, by the spirits of the departed.

But the remarkable fact remains that the village is far from being a united community. The unit of Nāga society is the Khel or sept, and each of these is in theory an exogamous group of brethren by blood at war with the rest of the world. Intense rivalry exists between the Khels of the same village; and though the feuds between each village and its neighbours, which in former times kept the whole country in a state of constant disturbance, have practically ceased since the British occupation, the quarrels between the Khels not infrequently result in riots and free-fights at the great drinking festivals. The Nāgas of North Kachār had a curious arrangement for mitigating the rancour caused by blood feuds. At stated times, once or twice a year, the whole village adjourned to a convenient place, and a general mêlée took place, every one fighting for his own hand. No weapons were used, but severe bruises were inflicted. These never gave cause for ill-feeling, whereas at other times the mere lifting of a hand would be a signal for a blood feud.

The Angāmis, according to Mr. Davis, have practically no religion, beyond a vague belief in a Supreme Creator, with which is combined the animistic worship of the spirits of trees, rocks, and pools of water.

The Aos are even ruder than the Angāmi branch of the Nāgas. 'Each of their villages,' says Mr. Davis, 'is a small republic, and each man is as good as his neighbour. Indeed, it would be hard to find anywhere more democratic communities. Head-men do exist, but their authority is small.' Before they came under British rule the Aos were notorious for the kidnapping of slaves, a habit which has been now almost entirely repressed. In the old days slaves were, it is said, generally kindly treated, being considered almost as members of the family; but those who were troublesome were sold to more distant and more savage tribes, among whom the custom of human sacrifice still persists. They were often made over by one village to another as a means of healing a feud, in satisfaction for any heads which might have been taken. 'Slaves paid in this way were invariably slaughtered by the village which received them, as an offering to the spirits of the men on their side who had been killed.'

The Semas, who are also included among the Nāgas, are even more savage than the Aos. Up to quite recent times they were ignorant of the use of money, and the custom of head-hunting prevailed among them. We see this practice in its most archaic form among the wilder tribes of Upper Burma, who are ethnically related to the hill-people of Assam. Their object in capturing the head of an enemy is to bring into subjection the spirit of the dead man, which is believed to accompany his skull to the home of the murderer. Hence, with a perfectly logical grasp of the situation, the skull of a stranger is preferred, because the spirit does not know its way in a strange land, and is therefore less likely to wander. Among the Nāgas, on the contrary, the habit arose from the much less primitive desire of acquiring a trophy.

Among the Nāga tribes the Semas were notorious for cruelty combined with treachery. It was considered by them praiseworthy to entertain a guest, and to slay him when he was off his guard. But all the Nāga tribes are, on occasion, head-hunters, and shrink from no treachery in securing these ghastly trophies. 'Any head counts,' says Mr. Davis, 'be it that of a man, woman, or child, and entitles the man who takes it to wear certain ornaments according to the custom of the tribe or village. Most heads are taken, or rather used to be taken, not in fair fight, but by methods the most treacherous. As common a method as any was for a man to lurk about the water Ghāt of a hostile village, and kill the first woman or child who came to draw water. Sometimes expeditions on a large scale were made, several villages combining for the sake of making a large bag. Even then, if the village to be attacked was found prepared, the valiant warriors who had come against it would, as a rule, retire without striking a blow. If, however, it was found that the whole adult population was away in the fields, an attack would be delivered, and as many children and old people as could within a reasonable time be killed would be killed, a retreat being effected before the men of the village attacked could have time to receive the news and return from their fields.'

Although these murderous raids have been to a large extent repressed, the desire for taking heads is still felt strongly by the younger generation. This is mainly the fault of the women who 'are given to laugh at the young bucks at the village festivals when they turn out without such decorations as mark the successful warrior.' This is the more remarkable, because in the old days when the business of head-hunting flourished, the women were usually the victims, because they were unarmed and unable to escape. It is noteworthy that among the Bhīls of the central hill tract the women were wont to protect the stranger, and resented any cruelty or licence on the part of the men.

The head-hunting and ruthless disregard of life which characterised the Nāgas naturally checked the social intercourse of the tribes. Among the allied villages, it is true, communications were admirably maintained by improving the hill paths and bridging the streams. But in other places the roads, sufficiently dangerous in themselves, were further interrupted by the savagery of the people. Dr. Grierson calls them 'a confused sample-bag of tribes,' among whom the extraordinary divergences of speech—differences of language, not merely of dialect—clearly reflect the reign of terror which the people have endured for countless generations. Thus Mr. Damant writes: 'Every tribe, almost every village is at war with its neighbour, and no Nāga of these parts dare leave the territory of his tribe without the probability that his life will be the penalty.' Within twenty miles of country five or six different dialects are often met with. Monosyllabic languages, like that of the Nāgas, possessing no literature and uncertain rules of pronunciation, are bound to change very rapidly and quite independently of each other. This process has been facilitated here by the savage manners of the race. The tattoo marks which each successful head-hunter is permitted to wear differ in pattern with each tribe, and, according to Mr. Peal, afford a means of recognising strangers. Without such marks and the use of gestures communication between branches of the tribe, each speaking a different language, would be impossible.

The Bachelors' Hall, known among the Nāgas as the Dekha-chang or Morang, is also found among the Dravidian tribes of the Bengal hills, among the Melanesians, and elsewhere. Only very young children live with their parents, the unmarried youths and girls sleeping in a separate house apart. The young men's hall is practically the village guardroom. It is built on a platform commanding an extensive view of all the approaches to the village. Here a sentry is always posted, who sounds the alarm by beating a hollow tree-trunk with a wooden mallet. This drum is often elaborately carved, like the figure-head of a ship, and usually represents the head of a buffalo which is curiously painted. In this hall are preserved the skulls of enemies taken in battle, and the inmates are in charge of the arms of the tribe, which they carefully clean and polish. Along both sides are the sleeping-berths of the young men, and the central space, floored with massive planks, is left open to be used by the braves in their dances. Outside are seats where the greybeards assemble in the evening to watch the youths practising running and putting the stone, amusements in which they delight. In the girls' house the maidens sleep two or three together, and sometimes an old woman is posted there as chaperon. But these precautions do not prevent free communication between the sexes.

The laws of the Nāgas regulating the Genna, or taboo, are most elaborate. These regulations enjoin the closing of the house or village, and are enforced on occasions of special manifestations of supernatural power, or when the gods are supposed to communicate directly with their worshippers. Thus a Genna is proclaimed in the event of an earthquake, eclipse, or the burning of a village. Such events are followed by the consultation of omens, and a special purgation is carried out in order to expel the evil spirits which are believed to be responsible for the occurrence. The village or house is then closed for two or three days, the inhabitants abstaining from all labour, and neither going out themselves nor permitting any stranger to enter during that period. The object of the rite seems to be to prevent the return of the evil spirits which have been so carefully expelled by the priest, and as taboo is infectious, the people of the house are required to remain in seclusion. Genna is also declared at the annual ceremony of making new fire for the village. A general sacrifice is offered, and the fire, when produced by friction, is first used in burning down the jungle for the sowing of the crops. Genna is also observed at the birth of a child, or even of any domestic animal, such as a cow or dog. Mr. Damant, the district officer, tells us that he was once refused a drink at a house because the dog had given birth to puppies. A similar taboo is enforced at the death of any important personage, the village being closed for two or three days, during which no one leaves or enters it. When the anger of the gods is believed to be specially manifested against a family—if, for instance, a member of it is drowned, crushed by a tree, or killed by a tiger—the household is compelled to resort to a remarkable rite of purification. They abandon their house with all the property which it contains. Everything they possess is destroyed by fire, and retaining only enough of clothing to cover their nakedness, they are compelled to wander in the jungle for a month, after which the anger of the gods is supposed to be appeased. The taboo extends even to the site of the house which they occupied, and when it is rebuilt a new place must be selected.

Though from the social point of view the Nāgas are in a state of savagery, they have in other ways attained a fairly high state of culture. Their agricultural knowledge is, as we have seen, higher than that of their neighbours, and their dress and arms exhibit some artistic taste and skill. They make a coarse cloth from the bark fibres of the nettle plant, and finer fabrics, curiously bordered and marked with triangular patches of red and black, are woven from the cotton which they grow. All their household vessels are of wood, which they carve with their Dao knives. Their spears and other arms are excellent specimens of metal-work. They make rough pottery, shaped by hand, without the use of the wheel. Their arms are a gleaming pole-axe with a short black handle, to which is hung a tuft of goat's hair dyed red; a broad-bladed spear, the shaft of which is covered with coloured hair like a brush; and a shield of buffalo hide. Their most important implement is the Dao, a heavy, short knife, which is used for a variety of purposes — in war, for carpentry and wood-carving, for felling jungle, and cutting firewood. They are adepts in laying out Pangis, sharpened stakes of bamboo, along the paths when they retreat before an enemy. The helmet, made of wicker-work or plaited cane, is conical in shape, about a foot high, and is covered with a layer of fur and hair, black or red in colour. Sometimes it is decorated with singular coronals made of pieces cut out of large shells, and on the crown is a little periwinkle-shaped basket-work cap, coloured black, with a scarlet border, and ornamented with peacocks' feathers and bunches of dyed wool. In front is a disc of polished brass and a crescent-shaped piece of buffalo horn. Warriors of distinction wear the hair of slain enemies hanging from the side ornaments of the helmet, and forming a fringe round the face. Women's tresses are preferred as being longer. The eastern Nāga warrior also wears a special collar on taking the first head. To this boar tusks are added to commemorate a second victim. After taking a third he may wear an apron covered with cowry shells arranged in a pattern which serves as a tally to mark the number of persons he has slain. One man showed to Mr. Carnegy his apron, which recorded the deaths of twenty-five individuals—men, women, and children—slain by his own hand. He was also entitled to fix in his hair one feather of the Dhanesh, or hornbill, for every man killed, and these were, with his other property, placed on his grave. The other drapery is scanty, and is replaced by a girdle of polished plates of brass with a kind of double stomacher above and below, or by a cuirass of hide with shoulder-pieces.

It is interesting to note among the eastern Nāgas the use of a kind of clan tartan. This cloth is made of cotton, dyed black with shades of red, blue, and green, arranged in stripes differing with different tribes. The pattern of the small apron worn by the Aos also differs from village to village. The hair decoration is equally distinctive. Among the eastern tribes in some septs the women, in others the men, use no clothing. 'The women's costume,' says Colonel Dalton, 'is simple, consisting of necklaces and an apron, or sometimes without the apron.' In North Kachār married women have a dress which distinguishes them from the maidens of the tribe. The former leave the bosom uncovered, while the latter wear a cloth tightly folded round the breast. The married women have their long hair plaited and knotted at the back, or sometimes flowing naturally over the shoulders. The unmarried girls have the hair cut square in front and brushed down over the forehead nearly to the eyebrows. Some of the men wear huge bunches of white cotton, as large as a man's fist, in their ears, which is said to give them a monkey-like appearance. Another remarkable portion of the Nāga wardrobe is a wooden tail, which among the Sema tribe is about eighteen inches long, and decorated with bunches of goat's hair dyed scarlet. According to Colonel Woodthorpe, 'all the Nāgas' personal decorations have a defensive purpose in view, like our old military stocks and epaulettes, and are planned to

Hindu Girl in the Plains

ward off the spear and axe, while the long hair which is so profusely used, waving about with every movement of the wearer, distracts the eye of the foe levelling a spear at him, and disturbs his aim.'

The Bhotiyas of North Assam retain more of the Mongoloid characteristics than the Nāgas. Their faces are broad and flat, eyes small and oblique, mouths large, noses short and low. At the same time many of the young women have fine, plump, rosy cheeks, 'healthy and pleasant,' says Colonel Dalton, 'to look on, though their complexions, a light olive, have nothing in common with the lily.' While the Nāgas are pure Animists, the Bhotiyas profess to be Buddhists, but this is only a veneer over the Animism which is their real belief. Polyandry is a recognised institution among them, and to quote the same writer: 'From my own observation, I believe the Bhotiyas to be utterly indifferent to the honour of their women, and the women themselves are devoid of delicacy and decency.' Their chief amusement is horse-racing, which is conducted in a remarkable way. At the starting-post all the riders dismount, and the ponies are flogged into a gallop by a gang of men armed with long whips. The rider holds on by the mane until the pony starts, and then is required to vault into his seat. No saddle or pad is allowed, and the contest is not so much a trial of the animal's speed as a test of the agility and horsemanship of the riders. It was from tribes skilled in this sport that polo was carried to Assam on the Burma frontier, whence it was adopted by Europeans.

Passing on from the Nāga, and Bhotiya tribes of Assam and its border, we have already noticed that in the western Himālayas the valleys open up easy routes to the mountainous hinterland. These entries must have been used by the Hindus of the plains from a very early time. This is shown by the sanctity attaching to this region, which appears in the earliest traditions of the race. In the Rāmāyana epic we read of the land of the Uttara Kurus, who are said to be liberal, prosperous, perpetually happy, and safe from the stroke of death. In this happy land, like the 'Island-valley of Avilion,' there is neither cold nor heat, no old age and disease, no grief and fear, no rain and sun. This tradition probably refers to the country north of Kashmir. The whole mountain region was regarded as the homes of the gods, and it contains some of the most sacred places of the Hindus. To this day crowds of pilgrims visit these inaccessible shrines, the merit being enhanced by the difficulties which attend the journey. The people of this region have none of the Nāga savagery, and during historical times have never raided the plains beneath them.

The greatest of these valleys is that of Kashmir, a basin surrounded by lofty mountains, and in the midst a fertile alluvial plain watered by the Jhelum and its tributaries. Mr. Drew's race map shows the wonderful mixture of races occupying the country. To the direct north, where recent expeditions have established the power of Kashmir at Gilgit, the most distant out-post of the Empire, we find Dards inhabiting the upper valley of the Indus. To the east and south come Baltis and Ladakhis. The valley itself is occupied by Kashmiris, with Pahāris to the south-east, and the outer ring of the hill-country is held by Chibhālis to the north and west, by Dogras to the east and south. We thus find, as might have been expected, the hinterland occupied by Mongoloid tribes, while the more accessible valleys are the home of races most of whom are immigrants from the plains.

To begin with the Dards to the north—the descriptions of them by Dr. Leitner and Mr. Drew make it clear that they are of the Aryan stock, broad-shouldered, stoutly built, and well proportioned; excellent mountaineers and hill porters, fairly good-looking, with hair which is sometimes black, sometimes brown. In complexion they are moderately fair, and the shade is sometimes light enough to allow the red to show through it. Their eyes are either brown or hazel. In what is called the Kohistān or hill-country, about the upper waters of the Indus, the people speak a Sanskritic tongue derived from the Indian plains, which in the region where the Pathāns are dominant has been replaced by Pashto. In spite of the rigour of the climate they are a bold, cheery, independent race. Like some of the Indo-Chinese people, they hold the cow in abhorrence. They will not use milk or butter, and even refuse to burn cow-dung, the common fuel of the East. Some cattle they are obliged to keep for ploughing, but they have as little as possible to do with them. When a cow calves they will put the calf to the udder by pushing it with a forked stick. But they will not touch it with their hands.

Further inland we meet three races of the Indo-Tibetan type—the Champas, who lead a nomadic life in the higher valleys, where no cultivation is possible, and the mode of life is purely pastoral; secondly, the Ladakhis, who are Tibetans settled in the main and side valleys of the Indus; thirdly, the Baltis, of the same stock as the Ladakhis, who have spread further down the Indus valley, and have been converted to Mohammedanism. These races bear in their appearance the stamp of their nationality. The Ladakhis are short in stature, with high cheek-bones, from which the face rapidly narrows downwards, and the chin is small and retreating. The most persistent peculiarity is that the outer corners of the eyes are drawn out, and the upper eyelids are overhung by a fold of the skin above them. Their eyes are brown in colour, and the nose as it were pressed into the face, and often depressed at the bridge. The mouth is large and inexpressive, the lips projecting, but not thick. Their black hair is cut close to the front and at the sides of the head; behind it is collected into a pigtail which reaches the small of the back. The beard and moustaches are scanty. The Champas and Baltis are of the same physical type. The former spend their lives in tents, wandering about with their flocks in search of pasturage as the snow yields to the increasing heat. The Baltis have now disused the pigtail, and partly follow the Mohammedan custom of shaving the head, only they leave side locks growing from behind the temples. This is the meeting ground of three religions—the Dards being Mohammedans, with outlying sections which follow Buddhism; the Ladakhis and Champas largely Buddhist; the Baltis have all adopted Islam.

In the inner ring of hills the Indo-Aryan element predominates. At the head are Brahmans and Rajputs, at the bottom the Dūms, a degraded race probably allied to the Doms of the plains. The valley population largely consists of fishermen and boatmen, who make their livelihood on the lakes and rivers. The races are here mixed and the types largely vary. Much has been said of the beauty of the women, but this does not depend so much on actual good looks as on their pretty rosy cheeks, which the man of the plains never sees at home and naturally admires. The Brahman lady is fair and delicate-looking; the Hānjni, or boatwoman, of a healthy red, both contrasting with the bolder and more exuberant charms of the Bātal dancing-girl, who dreads the camera least and is most generally photographed.

In Kulu and Kangra the Rajput is a good example of a state of society which is rapidly passing away. They are keenly jealous of their dignity, insisting on receiving a special form of salutation from those of a lower grade, the unauthorised assumption of which was in former days punished by fine and imprisonment. The Miān, or gentleman, who has been studied by Mr. Barnes, must observe four maxims—first, he must never drive the plough; secondly, he must never give his daughter in marriage to an inferior, nor marry himself below his rank; thirdly, he must never accept money in exchange for the betrothal of his daughter; lastly, his women must observe strict seclusion. The prejudice against the use of the plough, which is possibly due to the Buddhist regard for the sanctity of animal life, is the strongest of all, and any one offending in this way is excluded from the society of his equals. They may be recognised by their emaciated looks and coarse clothes, and they are in a state of wretched poverty while the abundant vacant land around them lies ready for the plough. 'Some,' says Mr. Barnes, 'lounge away their time on the tops of the mountains, spreading nets for the capture of hawks; many a day they watch in vain, subsisting on berries and on game accidentally entangled in their nets. At last, when fortune grants them success, they despatch the prize to their friends below, who tame and instruct the bird for the purpose of sale. Others will stay at home, and pass their time sporting either with a hawk, or, if they can afford it, with a gun. One Rajput beats the bushes, and the other carries the hawk ready to spring upon any quarry that rises to the view. At the close of the day, if they have been successful, they exchange the game for a little meal, and thus prolong existence over another span. The marksman armed with a gun will sit up for wild pigs returning from the fields, and in the same manner barter their flesh for other necessaries of life. However, the prospect of starvation has already driven many to take the plough, and the number of seceders daily increases. Our administration, though just and liberal, has a levelling tendency. Service is no longer to be procured, and to many the stern alternative has arrived of taking to agriculture and securing comparative comfort, or enduring the pangs of hunger and death. So long as any resource remains the fatal step will be postponed, but it is easy to see that the struggle cannot be long protracted. Necessity is a hard taskmaster, and sooner or later the pressure of want will inevitably overcome the scruples of the most bigoted.'

This account gives a lively picture of the unavailing struggle of a proud race, whose position depends upon status, with advancing industrialism.

The lower castes in this region, Rathis, Chiraths, and Kanets, are in many cases Rajputs who have fallen in the world and have taken to a life of agriculture.

Two races connected with this region in the western hills deserve special mention—the Nāgas and the Khasas.

The true character of the Nāgas, who must be carefully distinguished from the race of the same name in Assam, can hardly be disentangled from the mass of legend with which they are surrounded. One branch of them, according to Hindu belief, was created to people Patāla, or the underworld, where they still reign in splendour. An ancient poem describes the city of the Nāga Rāja, which 'contained two thousand millions of serpent inhabitants, all of whose wives were of surpassing beauty. The city supplied more jewels than any person in the world has ever seen, and there was a lake there in which flowed the water of life, in which all the serpents used to bathe.' In short, it was in the Land of Faery. The other, the terrestrial branch, is said to have occupied a large part of Northern India in prehistoric times. Dr. Oldham has recently, without much success, attempted to show that they and the Asuras, a kindred people, were a non-Aryan race which opposed the Aryans, and that the deified Nāgas are the sainted ancestors of this people. All that can be said with confidence about this people is that they were probably serpent worshippers, and the legends indicate a struggle between some form of Hinduism and this belief. It has been suspected that the myths speak of a contest of Aryan *versus* Mongolian; but it is impossible to say whether the Nāgas constituted an ethnical group or were merely an aggregate of more than one tribe united by a common faith.

It is different with the Khasas, who certainly appear to be one of the Aryan tribes driven by later immigrants to take shelter in the hills. Their successors are the Khasiyas of Kumaun, the hill-country which borders Nepal on the west. They always profess to be Rajputs who have fallen from their original high estate through living in a land where the usages of orthodox Hinduism were neglected. Their isolation in this hill-country doubtless caused laxity of religious practice; but since Kumaun has been opened out they are gradually assimilating their usages to those of the orthodox Hindu of the plains.

East of Kumaun lies Nepal, which is interesting as the home of the Gurkhas, perhaps the finest infantry in our Indian army Here the seclusion enforced by its jealous rulers renders ethnological inquiry most difficult. But the investigations of Dr. Oldfield, Colonel Waddell, and Mr. Gait, who have continued the work begun by Mr. Hodgson, throw some light on the facts. The Newārs, which form the bulk of the people, are partly Mongoloid, partly Aryan. The ruling dynasty has sprung from a small gang of military adventurers, Rajput immigrants from the plains. The Khas, a branch of the Khasas already described, are the most Hinduised element, and supply the majority of officers to the local army. The Gurkha, Mangar, and Gurung furnish recruits to our regiments. The present rulers pretend to an exaggerated standard of Hindu orthodoxy, rigidly enforce the Hindu law, and strictly prohibit the slaughter of cows. But the religion of the lower classes is Hinduism tempered by survivals of an earlier animistic cult. Caste rules sit lightly upon them, and in particular they violate Hindu rules in the matter of food and drink. It is this freedom from caste restrictions which makes the Gurkha so valuable as a soldier. He has none of the conventions which rule the sepoy from the plains. He troubles little about his commissariat, and hence is on much more friendly terms with the British soldier than the ordinary sepoy. Most Gurkhas at home eat the meat of buffaloes and sheep as well as pork, and care little about ceremonial ablutions. The Newārs and their more Mongoloid kinsmen add to this diet the flesh of goats and fowls. The highest Nepalese, according to Colonel Waddell, will take water from the hands of the pork-eating Bhotiyas, an act which would scandalise even the meanest orthodox Hindu.

The last portion of the northern barrier is the north-western frontier, extending from the northern point of the Punjab to the Arabian Sea. Here three races stand out prominently—the Pathān or Afghān to the north, the Baloch and Brahui to the south. These peoples, while displaying a somewhat general uniformity of character and ways of life, differ widely in their social organisation. The facts have been admirably examined by Mr. Hughes-Buller, whose essay deserves attentive study as one of the most original contributions to Indian ethnology in modern times.

The Afghān tribe is based on the principle of kinship; that is to say, it is composed of a number of kindred groups of agnates, who reckon descent through the father. But its constitution admits of association within the tribe of a certain number of alien groups, who are said 'to live within its shade.' These are foreign allies introduced for active participation in any blood feud which the tribe may have on hand. On the other hand, the tribe is subject to constant loss by fission, when, in consequence of their nomadic habits, one section breaks off and abandons the common land and water. This severance may be temporary or permanent, and in the latter case the independent group sets up for itself.

Among the Baloch the organisation is much looser. There is no eponymous ancestor, and the tribe itself does not profess to be homogeneous. Outsiders from all quarters are freely admitted to membership as valuable allies to be used in the constant blood feuds in which the tribes are engaged. When such an outsider

No. 6

Women in the Plains, showing Dress and Jewellery

shows his worth he is assigned a share in the tribal lands, and intermarries within the tribe. The Baloch are now gradually changing their mode of life from the nomadic to the pastoral. Their chief usually has a fixed residence, but this never becomes the nucleus of a town. Most of them live in the country, where their villages are collections of mud or stone walls, over which temporary roofs are erected. When the community moves to another grazing-ground the roofs are carried off, and the walls are left for the accommodation of the next comers. In some cases they live in recesses or ledges of the cliffs. Their wealth consists in cattle, camels, sheep, and goats; but arts, such as embroidery and carpet-making, flourish among them, as with the Turkomans, with whom they must at some time in their history have been in contact. Robbers they were and are, save so far as these pursuits have been restricted under British rule. Their mode and ideals of life were thus expressed by one of these tribes: 'We are the enemies of all our neighbours. We do no good to any one, and nobody wishes us well. Let us afford every encouragement to strife around us; let us give passage through our country to any neighbour who seeks to injure another. It matters not to us which side is injured or destroyed; in any case we shall be the gainers.'

The Afghāns to be seen in the Indian plains are largely Ghilzais, Turks by race, introduced into the country within historical times, and not akin to the Afghāns except in language and religion. Their

Kāfilas, or caravans, laden with cloth, fruits, and accompanied by live-stock in the shape of horses and Persian cats, traverse the northern plains during the cold season. They are big, burly men, dirty in person and dress, and with a profound contempt for the Hindu, except the Sikh, whom they respect as their national enemy. They are accomplished horse-copers, and no Yorkshireman understands better how to pass off an unsound animal on an unwary purchaser.

Wilder even than the Baloch are the Pathān tribes of the north-west frontier. From their almost impregnable strongholds in the overhanging mountains they have for ages been accustomed to harry the plains with impunity. They nominally follow the creed of the Prophet, but pay more regard to local saints whose intercession they consider efficacious. No people with whom the British have dealings are more faithless than these frontier Pathāns. No promise, no oath binds them. 'Keep a cousin poor, but use him; when he is little play with him; when he is grown up he is a cousin, fight him,' is one of their common proverbs. At the same time the Pathān, as Sir D. Ibbetson points out, has a code of morality of his own, which includes three obligations—the right of asylum, which compels him to shelter and protect even an enemy who comes as a suppliant; the necessity of revenge by retaliation; open-handed hospitality to all who may demand it. Of these three perhaps the last is greatest. The Pathān, says the proverb, is at one moment a saint, at another a devil. 'For centuries he has been, on our frontier at least, subject to no man. He leads a free, wild, active life in the rugged fastnesses of his mountains; and there is an air of masculine independence about him which is refreshing in a country like India. He is a bigot of the most fanatical type, exceedingly proud, and extraordinarily superstitious. He is of stalwart make, and his features are often of a markedly Semitic type. His hair, plentifully oiled, hangs long and straight to his shoulder; he wears a loose tunic, baggy drawers, a sheet or blanket, sandals, and a sheepskin coat with its wool inside. His favourite colour is a dark blue, and his national arms the long, heavy, Afghan knife, and the matchlock or Jazail. His women wear a loose shift, wide wrinkled drawers down to their ankles, and a wrap over the head; and are, as a rule, jealously secluded. Both sexes are filthy in their persons.' At the same time there is a charm about them, and they have a romantic side to their character. They alternate, as Mountstuart Elphinstone said, desperate forays with strains that might have tuned a shepherd's pipe. In short, they are not to be judged by the laws which regulate the lives of civilised people. From their own point of view they are soldiers of fortune who, in order to secure their freedom, have been compelled to resort to methods which are inconsistent with the principles under which our rule of the settled villages on their border must be conducted.

To the north of the Peshawar valley lies a region as yet imperfectly explored. It is a paradise to the ethnologist, the one part of the borderland where important discoveries will certainly be made when the fierce tribes which now occupy it have been reduced to order. It contains extensive Buddhist remains which will throw light on the early history of that faith. Of the Kāfirs, for instance, among whom some survivals of Greek culture have been recognised, we possess, in spite of the researches of Dr. Leitner and Sir G. Robertson, only imperfect knowledge. In this wild region there are, says Mr. Oliver, 'societies given to drinking wine and making merry, who lay down cellars of clarified butter, and do not consider it ripe till it has acquired the deep red of a century's keeping; with whom dancing is for both sexes the national amusement, and polo the national game; who still practise the ordeal of fire'; and are quite free from jealousy regarding the honour of their women. But this borderland lies beyond the limits of this sketch.

A PANKA, DRAVIDIAN WEAVER, SOUTHERN HILLS (p. 136)

CHAPTER IV

THE TRIBES OF THE SOUTHERN HILLS

Kolis: Bhīls: Gonds. Status of the hill tribes. Conversion to Hinduism. Oraons: Kols: Mundas: Paharias: Santāls.

IN the Dravidian area, including the forest region of Northern Bombay, the Central India Agency, the Central Provinces, and the hilly tracts of the United Provinces, and Bengal, the condition of things is very different from that of the Himālayan region. The hills are much lower and more accessible, and the tribes nowhere display that degree of savagery and independence which characterises the Nāgas or Pathāns.

From the Gulf of Cambay on the west to that point in the Bengal delta where the hill-country projects into the valley of the Ganges, we have at least three groups, which, though geographically distinct, are of a fairly uniform ethnological type—Kolis and Bhīls to the west; Gonds, Korkus, and Baigas in the centre; to the east, Oraons, Mundas, and Santāls. These are again philologically divided into the Munda-speaking and Dravidian-speaking tribes, both languages being more or less influenced by the Aryan tongues of the north. All along this range of hill-country the character, institutions, religion, and modes of life differ in a remarkable way according to the extent to which they have been modified by the Hindu races in the Ganges valley and Rajputana.

To the west the broken Koli and Bhīl tribes, which occupy a region exposed to the march of invaders pressing from the north into the Deccan, have preserved little individuality. Though at times they have been notorious for brigandage, and even now occasionally commit gang robberies and thefts of cattle, none of these people exhibit savagery of the Himālayan type. Raiding for slaves and heads is unknown, and since the British have occupied their country they have seldom caused trouble to the authorities. The Gonds of the Central Provinces have come within the range of Hindu influence only in quite recent years. When the Central Provinces were first formed into a separate administration in 1861, the earliest comprehensive account of what had hitherto been an unknown land was supplied in the famous report by Sir R. Temple. Since that time the construction of roads and railways, and the growth of a vast trade in cereals, cotton, and forest produce have brought the Gonds, Korkus, and allied tribes within the pale of civilisation. They have become more and more subject to Hindu influence from the north, and are rapidly losing those primitive manners and customs which made the study of them so interesting to the ethnologist. This is also the case in varying degrees with the tribes lying further east. Nowhere, except in the plateau of Chota Nagpur and the wild country south of it, where the compact tribal organisation of the people and the inaccessibility of their settlements have protected them from intrusion, does the primitive type survive uninfluenced by Aryan culture from the north.

Some of these tribes, or some of their septs, to whom reference is here made, lie south of the Nerbudda, the boundary of the races comprehended in this sketch. But it is impossible to describe them without occasionally overstepping a frontier which is neither ethnical nor linguistic.

If we start from the Gulf of Cambay on the west, the first important tribe which we encounter is that of the Kolis, who in this part of the country number one and three-quarter millions. They may be divided into two branches—the coast men and the hillmen. The former, doubtless in consequence of intermixture with some foreigners, such as the Arabs, the chief mercantile people of the western ocean, are a stronger, sturdier race than the hillmen, and some of their women are remarkably fair-complexioned and handsome. They are excellent seamen, and furnish many Lascars to our mercantile marine. But their chief occupation is catching fish for the Bombay market. They use several kinds of boats and nets suited to the conditions of the tidal and deep-sea fisheries. In every sound and creek the path which fish are likely to take is barred by rows of stakes, between which, as the tide begins to rise, the nets are set, and hauled when the tide is at its height. The fishermen are a tall, muscular race, whose chief fault is that they are rather given to drink and to quarrels when in their cups. The hillmen were long notorious as hereditary, professional plunderers, 'soldiers of the night,' as they used to call themselves. The earliest annals of the country tell how one of the Rajput overlords who invaded these districts from the north endeavoured to reduce them to order. But his measures failed, and all his successors have been forced to undertake the same irksome task. In 1804 Colonel Wallace reported that 'most Kolis are thieves by profession, and embrace every opportunity of plundering both public and private property. It is these habits, contrasted with the obsequious character of the rest of the inhabitants, that has given rise to the names Rāsti or peaceful, and Mehvās or faithless.' But they have never shown any capacity of uniting for a common object, and even in the good old days of freedom they were often led by foreigners, renegade Rajputs, who joined the jungle folk, and have given names to many of their septs. Nowadays they have taken to labour and farming in a fitful way, and though it is necessary to watch them, brigandage has practically ceased.

Further east come the Bhīls, who number nearly one and a quarter millions. According to local tradition they were once the ruling race in Rajputana, Central India, and Gujarat, and it is believed that they, like the Kolis, were reduced to subjection by the Rajput tribes, who from the end of the fifth century of our era began to push their way southwards. In many of the states of Rajputana, Malwa, and Gujarat this claim is recognised by their overlords, and whenever a Rajput chief succeeds to the throne, it is a necessary part of the rite of investiture that his brow should be marked with blood drawn from the thumb or toe of a Bhīl. He thus becomes admitted by the covenant of blood into the kin of the ancient rulers of the land.

The appearance of the Bhīl tribes, scattered over the hill-country of Rajputana and the forests north of the Nerbudda, indicates that they include the members of more than one broken, lawless people who were driven to the hills by later settlers, while some remained as serfs in the lowlands. We reach the same result on the linguistic evidence. Their original Dravidian tongue seems to have entirely disappeared, and they now speak, in some thirty dialects, a language intermediate between those of Gujarat and Rajputana, obviously borrowed from the newcomers. It is one of the curiosities of Indian philology that Dr. Grierson has discovered a small tribe of thieves in Orissa, a thousand miles distant from the true home of the race, speaking a Bhīl dialect. They seem to have left their country for their country's good during Mahratta rule some five or six generations ago.

In the jungles of Khandesh, the Bombay district south of the Nerbudda, they have been described as active and hardy, with high cheek-bones, wide nostrils, and coarse, almost Negroid features, all indications of pure Dravidian blood. Those of the plains are often well built, of tall stature and handsome features, with wavy hair, the original stock being here obviously combined with an Aryan strain.

The hill Bhīls retain, or did so till quite recently, many old-world customs and beliefs. They occupy the primitive round, hive-like huts, with a narrow doorway through which the inmates creep for shelter. These huts are hastily erected on the crests of the hills, to which their builders occasionally resort in search of game and jungle produce. When disease appears, the site is supposed to be spirit-haunted and unlucky, and it is immediately abandoned. Thus they suffer much less from epidemics than the settled population of the plains. Their clothing is of the most meagre kind, but its scantiness is supplemented by the abundance of the coarse jewellery in which they delight. They live mainly on what the forest supplies, and they have all the thriftlessness, love of ardent spirits, gaiety, simplicity, honesty, and detestation of honest work which characterise the true savage.

They amuse themselves with wild jungle dances, in which the men dress as women, or imitate various animals, bounding backwards and forwards to the music of their rude instruments, among which a sort of bagpipe is most popular.

Their religion is a gross form of Animism, which needs no temple and no regular priest. Sometimes they raise a flimsy shed over some specially holy stone; more usually a few water-worn pebbles piled beneath a shady tree serve as their place of worship. They believe strongly in witchcraft, and their Barvas, or witch-finders, are supposed to possess the hereditary gift of inspiration, which is indicated by a sort of shamanistic frenzy. As the officiant listens to the wild songs in honour of the spirits of hill, or tree, or spring, the god comes upon him, and he dances with frantic

BAĪSWĀRS, DRAVIDIAN CULTIVATORS, SOUTHERN HILLS (p. 21)

gestures, his long hair floating behind him, until he faints from sheer exhaustion. While in this ecstatic state their inarticulate utterances are regarded as oracles, foretelling the prospects of the season, or foreboding disease and other calamities which are invariably attributed to evil spirits.

On special occasions they practise the rite of fire-walking, which seems to be confined throughout India to the non-Aryan races. A sacrifice is offered, the priest or medicine-man mutters an incantation, waves a naked sword over the fire to scare the spirit which would scorch the performers, and then calls upon a Bhīl to walk through a trench filled with blazing charcoal. A European observer who witnessed the rite satisfied himself that the man escaped injury. But as the same result followed when his Mohammedan orderly made the attempt, it is clear that no special protective was used. It has been suggested that the performer secures immunity by resting his feet on the cooler ashes or on the sides of the trench, or that the spectators are under some influence of the hypnotic kind. The methods and objects of fire-walking in India are little known because the rite is practised in secret and among secluded tribes. It deserves more careful scientific investigation than has hitherto been bestowed upon it.

But though the customs and mode of life of the hill Bhīls are distinctly savage, their tribal organisation seems to be efficient. Each tribe has a hereditary chief, who before the advent of British rule exercised the powers of life and death, and is still treated with much respect. He is aided by a hereditary minister, who is also a Bhīl, and these two officials, acting on the advice of a council of greybeards, manage all their affairs. In the plains this system has been replaced by the ordinary Hindu low caste panchayat or tribal council, which is appointed not for a single village, but for an extensive tract of country under the control of a head-man, who, when necessary, convenes the council for the despatch of business. All matters of social or religious importance are settled in this way, and the Bhīl, on account of his criminal proclivities, is shy in appealing to British courts of justice.

East of the Bhīl and Koli country is that of the Gonds, who number more than two and a quarter millions. They are remarkable as being the only Dravidian race in Northern India which founded kingdoms and established a polity of its own. The rise of these kingdoms, which were the work of three princely houses, Garha-Mandla, Deogarh, and Chanda, all now included in the Central Provinces, dates from the sixteenth century. Their foundation was possible just at this time because they were established after the destruction of the Hindu dynasties of Northern India by the Mohammedans, and before the latter power seriously interfered in Deccan politics. In the interval the Moghul, from his palaces at Agra and Delhi, looked with contempt on these jungle princelets, from whom he required only nominal submission. In the end they were overwhelmed by the new Mahratta power.

We know little of their system of government, which

seems to have been of the semi-feudal type, the authority of the local chiefs being maintained, and a small tribute and a supply of recruits for the royal army being the only service required from them. Under their rule the country prospered. An English traveller, whose contemporary account is unfortunately anonymous, writes: 'Without the benefit of navigation—for the Nerbudda is here not navigable—and without much inland commerce, but under the fostering hand of a race of Gond princes, a numerous people tilled a fertile country, and still preserve in the neatness of their houses, in the number and magnificence of their temples, in the size of their towns, and the frequency of their plantations, the undoubted signs of enviable prosperity.' Then came the Mahratta invasion, the occupation of the country by a people who wrecked the indigenous civilisation, and left ruin and misery in their train. They dealt with the jungle-folk in their usual ruthless fashion, and when the British came upon the scene they found the Gonds ejected from their holdings in the plains, and driven into the jungles of the Satpura and Mahadeo ranges, which they now occupy undisturbed.

The northern branch of the Gonds has been fully described by Mr. Hislop and Captains Forsyth and Ward. Mr. Hislop speaks of them as 'a little below the average height generally of Hindus; bodies well proportioned, but features rather ugly—a roundish head, distended nostrils, wide mouths, straight black hair, and scanty beard and moustaches'—all Dravidian characteristics. Captain Ward describes the wild

Gonds of Mandla as well behaved and amenable to authority. They are occasionally addicted to cattle-lifting, but considering the facility with which this crime could be committed and concealed, it is wonderful that the cases are not more numerous. 'The Gond in service,' he writes, 'is exceptionally faithful and obedient to his employer, so much so that he would not hesitate to commit any crime at his orders, and sooner than turn informer would himself die. This description applies only to the really wild Gonds who have not become contaminated by contact with spurious civilisation, for the domesticated Gond is mean, cringing, cowardly, and as great a liar as any other low class of Indian.'

Under favourable circumstances—that is to say, when they are well fed—Gonds are strong and well proportioned, though slightly built, very expert with the axe, and though lazy, do not make bad farm-servants. The Mari Gonds of Bastar, further south, were, when they were first observed by Captain Glasfurd, of a much more primitive type. They had the greatest fear of a horse, or of an unusual number of persons suddenly coming upon their villages. Captain Glasfurd, in order to gain their confidence, was obliged to leave his camp and approach their neighbourhood with as few attendants as possible. When he came near he used to dismount, take a guide from the more civilised branch of the tribe; thus only could he ensure that the wild men would not escape into the jungles. He found their flimsy huts to be made of grass daubed over with mud, and the clothing of both sexes was of the scantiest kind. They grew a little coarse grain on the hill-slopes, but had no buffaloes, oxen, or cows. Therefore, in the absence of a plough, they cultivated their land in a most imperfect fashion by means of a long-handled hoe; but even this they used only in the better fields where they grew tobacco and castor. For the inferior crops they practised the usual method of burning patches of jungle.

Among the true Gonds, the Baigas of Mandla, the rough country on the left bank of the Nerbudda, hold the highest rank, and supply priests to the whole tribe. They differ in appearance from the true Gonds—the head is longer, the nose more aquiline, and the hands peculiarly small. This would seem to indicate a strain of Aryan blood. They are fearless, trustworthy, and independent. Their social life is carefully regulated by their own tribal council. They are slight, wiry, hardy men, and excellent sportsmen. Cunning in making traps and pitfalls, and capital shots with bow and arrow, they soon clear a country of game. When an animal is wounded they never quit the trail, and the poison, *nux vomica* soaked in cotton and tied to the barb, is so deadly that the beast struck is certain to die sooner or later. Unarmed, save with a tiny axe, they wander through the densest jungle. The speed with which they ascend trees on an alarm of tigers is wonderful. But on an emergency they stand by their comrades in a most courageous way. Their skill with the axe is remarkable, and by flinging it they kill peacocks, small deer, hares, and even leopards. On these hunting expeditions, which often last three or four days, they subsist almost altogether on what they kill, or on the roots and fruits found in the forests. They cultivate a little grain in the most thriftless way.

The condition of many of these jungle tribes is miserable and degraded, but at the same time their status is far superior to that of the menial castes in the plains. Many of the latter are regarded as so foul in the eyes of orthodox Hindus that their touch causes pollution. But the unkempt, semi-naked Gond or Bhīl suffers from no taboo of this kind. He regards himself as a free gentleman of the forest, and when he meets the Hindu and accepts his culture or religion as a substitute for his own, he does so without any admission of inferiority. This fact has been well illustrated for the Central Provinces by Mr. Russell, who points out that these tribes were never so fully subjugated as were the northern Dravidians of the plains. They were never completely ousted from possession of the land, and they still maintain in many places the status of landlords. In fact, the Aryan migration to this part of the country was even more clearly than in the north one of colonisation rather than of conquest. It would also seem that these hill Dravidians were not condemned to discharge the meaner industries—those of the mat-maker, cane-worker, currier, washerman, and scavenger—probably because menials from the north, who have already specialised these industries, accompanied the colonists. It was at a late period of their history that the Aryans came in contact with these jungle-folk. The former had long been settled in the Gangetic valley, and had thus become more tolerant of people whose skins were darker than their own. Thus they gradually ceased to regard them with the horror which the first Aryans exhibited towards the Dasyus. By this time there had been a certain amount of interbreeding and admission of the Dravidian groups into the inner circles of Hinduism, and race distinctions had come to be merged in the gradations of caste and occupation.

The process by which tribes like these become assimilated to Hindus has been often described by Sir A. Lyall and other writers. The ascetic orders have provided the agency by which many such people have been converted. The Hindu missionary starts his work among the leading men of the tribe, and hints that it is no longer creditable that worthy people like themselves should cling to their foul habits of eating, and neglect the requirements of personal purity. He does not encourage them to abandon at once the tribal deities; rather, the more respectable of these are gradually adopted into the Hindu pantheon as incarnations of one or other of the greater Hindu gods. Meanwhile the old gods are not quite neglected. They continue to be worshipped habitually by women, and occasionally by men when serious trouble overtakes them. When the jungle man nominally accepts Hinduism, he is obliged to undertake none of the onerous duties of the new religion, nor does he abandon the course of life to which he is accustomed. All he need do is to keep a Brahman chaplain, who will act as his family priest, and vicariously perform the needful rites on behalf of his employer. Such a man by and by becomes ashamed to be known as a Gond or Bhīl, and he blossoms out into the leader of a new Rajput sept, in the sense that, like the true Rajput of the plains, he is the cadet of a ruling race. Of course, he is not at once admitted to marriage rights by genuine Rajputs. But if the candidate for promotion is only rich enough and persistent in urging his claims, this boon is granted sooner or later, and the social status of the chief and his tribesmen becomes finally assured.

It is only in the plateau of Chota Nagpur that the Dravidians have resisted Hindu influence of this kind. As examples of such tribes we may take the Oraons, Kols, and Santāls, who have been fully described by Colonel Dalton, Sir W. Hunter, and Messrs. Bartley-Birt and Risley.

The Oraons, whose name is probably derived from the Dravidian *horo*, 'man,' which under other forms gives a title to the Hos and Kols, are apparently the earliest settlers in the plateau which they now occupy. Their colour is the darkest brown, approaching black; the hair jet black, coarse, and rather inclined to be frizzly. 'Projecting jaws and teeth, thick lips, low narrow foreheads, broad flat noses, are the features,' according to Mr. Risley, 'which strike a careful observer as characteristic of the tribe. The eyes are often bright and full, and no obliquity is observable in the opening of the eyelids. No signs of Mongolian affinities can be detected in the relative positions of the malar and nasal bones.'

Mānjhi Cultivators, Southern Hills, with Sacred Drum (p. 21)

They must be classed, therefore, as pure-blooded Dravidians, and though living in a country where the Munda, or as it used to be called the Kolarian speech, is used, they preserve the Dravidian Kurukh dialect almost unchanged. In their dress they attach particular importance to the girdle of cord or cane fibre, which is now of no practical use, but represents a survival of a more primitive costume, like that of the Juāngs, a kindred tribe, who employ it to support the fig-leaf which constitutes their wardrobe.

Their marriage customs are most primitive. The youths, like those of the Nāgas, are supposed to sleep in a bachelors' hall; but the intercourse of the sexes is practically unrestricted, ante-nuptial connections are the rule rather than the exception, and marriage, as they understand the term, is equivalent to cohabitation. 'To call this state of things immoral,' says Mr. Risley, 'is to apply a modern conception to primitive habits of life. Within the tribe, indeed, the idea of sexual morality seems hardly to exist, and the unmarried Oraons are not far from the conditions of modified promiscuity which prevails among many of the Australian tribes. At the same time intrigues beyond the limits of the tribe are uncommon, and are punished by summary expulsion.'

In the eyes of the Hindu the Oraon is naturally quite outside the bounds of the caste system. He continues to eat, as his forefathers did, almost anything that comes in his way—beef, pork, fowls, fish, alligators, lizards, field-rats, and even the flesh of animals which have died a natural death. This is the diet of the foul, menial castes in the Bengal plains, like the Bagdis, Doms, or Bauris. But as is the case in the Central Provinces, the Oraon is regarded, not as an outcast who has fallen below the standard of life imposed by the laws of caste, but rather as an outsider who has never been included in the Hindu system and owes no allegiance to it.

The Kols and Mundas of Chota Nagpur are, except the Hos and Santāls, the finest specimens of these hill-people. They average about 5 feet 6 inches in height, and their open-door life and exposure to all kinds of weather keep them in a hard condition well adapted for sustaining long and arduous exertion. 'Their skin,' writes Mr. Bradley-Birt, 'is of the darkest brown, almost black in many cases, and their features coarse, with broad flat noses, low foreheads, and thick lips, presenting as a rule a by no means prepossessing appearance. The women are often more pleasing, the coarseness of their features less accentuated or less noticeable on account of the extreme good-nature and happy carelessness that seldom fail to mark their countenances.'

The last refuge of the hill Dravidians is in that upland so graphically described by Mr. Bradley-Birt, which projects like an arm or peninsula from the Rajmahāl hills. 'To the south this rugged range sinks gradually to meet the plains. To the north the Ganges cuts it abruptly in full height, bringing it up sharply face to face with the rice fields of Bengal that lie in all their fertile luxuriance upon its northern bank. It is the meeting-place of the old and new, the river circling round the foot of the hills as if to cut it off from the progress that has marked the more accessible lands that lie beyond. Steep, rocky, and inaccessible, clothed in dense scrub jungle, the passing of the centuries has left little mark on the Rajmahāl hills. They stand almost as wild and untouched to-day as when the earliest of the hillmen who still prefer them came in the long-forgotten past and took possession.'

The first occupants of this inhospitable, secluded region were the Dravidian Paharias or 'hillmen,' a name which must have been given to them by their Aryan neighbours in the plains below. They are the wildest and most backward of the Bengal aborigines. They have no tradition of their origin ; but it has been supposed that they were gradually pushed eastward by the pressure of other tribes, until they were brought to a stand in the hilly *cul de sac* where the British found them in occupation when they conquered the country. This wild tract of hill and forest offered them an impregnable sanctuary, and supplied from its game and jungle produce all their simple wants. But, like eagles looking down from an aerie on a mountain cliff, they commanded the great trade route along the valley of the Ganges, and for many centuries they plundered and harried the rear-guard of armies, the trading caravans, and the fertile villages which lay exposed to their attacks. Even the powerful Moghul dared not interfere with this nest of caterans, and it was left to a British officer, Augustus Cleveland, at the end of the eighteenth century, to reduce them to order by a policy of tactful conciliation.

In physique, manners, and customs the Paharias, known also as the Mal or Malē, are closely connected with the Oraons. Their religion is of the animistic type, the head of their pantheon being Dharmer Gossain, the sun god, and beneath him a host of minor gods to each of whom some department of human affairs is assigned. Thus, one presides over strong drink, another over highways, a third over hunting, a fourth guards the central pole of the hut. This is a decided advance on the theology of the Oraons, who recognise only an ill-defined group of spirits, generally hostile to men, to each of whom no special function is appointed. It is doubtful if the Paharias have any priests, their place being taken by the Demāno, or sorcerer. In their way of life they follow the rudest aboriginal model. They cling to the rough, inaccessible country in which they live, where they carry on a rude jungle husbandry. Like the Oraons, they have no restrictions in the matter of food, and eat anything edible which they can procure.

Within the range of hills occupied by the Paharias is a sort of enclave of undulating land, once covered with jungle, but containing rich stretches of fertile soil. This tract, known as the Dāman-i-Koh, the skirt of the hills, was unoccupied when the British entered into possession. They offered it to the Paharias, and used every means to induce them to settle within it. But with the conservatism of the true jungle-dweller, they steadily refused to abandon their original hill settlements, and the task of clearing this district was left to another and a more enterprising people.

These were the Santāls, a race of pure Dravidian blood, whose strange and eventful history supplies one of the great precedents which have ever since defined the relations of the Indian Government with the aboriginal tribes. We know little of their early history and migrations. They have, it is true, a curiously elaborate collection of cosmogonies and tribal legends, which in themselves form a most interesting study. These abound in geographical names, but unfortunately few of them can now be identified with certainty. We may conclude with some degree of confidence that, like the Paharias, they came from the west. It is possible that the growing numbers of the Santāls and deficient means of support may have forced them to migrate eastward. Or this may have been the result of pressure from the Gonds or other western races. At any rate, when they first came under observation they were established in Hazāribāgh, one of the districts of Chota Nagpur lying south of the cities of Patna and Gaya. There they seem to have come into conflict with the Birhors, another Dravidian tribe, and they were again driven further east towards the river Damuda. On its banks they must have settled for a long period, because it became the sacred river of the race, and to this day the ashes of their dead are consigned to its waters. Early in the nineteenth century this eastward movement continued, and they appeared in the neighbourhood of the Dāman-i-Koh in 1832. It offered them the asylum which they needed, and from the Paharias, to whom the reversion of this district should naturally have fallen, they had no reason to expect opposition.

The Santāls were distinguished from the other kindred Dravidian tribes by their strong national feeling and by their determination to preserve themselves from contamination by foreign races. They cleared the rich red soil of the land which had fallen to their lot, and while the Paharias on the slopes overhanging the valley continued the ancient system of jungle tillage, the Santāls dug irrigation channels and covered their territory with rice fields. As they prospered and multiplied misfortune overtook them. Dress and jewellery, marriage and death rites became more expensive, and they gradually fell under the yoke of the Hindu money-lenders from the plains, who swindled them and took mortgages on their holdings and crops until they were reduced to a condition little better than that of serfs. The Indian Government at the time was engrossed in the struggle with the Mahrattas and Sikhs. Little was known of the economical position of the Santāls, and British courts of law were allowed to give effect to the fraudulent engagements between the money-lender and the hillman.

In the period just before the Mutiny of 1857 matters reached a crisis. About this time the construction of railways in the Ganges valley began. There is no better navvy than the Santāl, and the impoverished hillmen flocked to the works. Those who obtained employment soon returned with well-lined pockets, and the contrast of the riches of the workman with the poverty of those who stayed at home only served to aggravate the discontent. The result was the Santāl insurrection of 1854, when a people driven to despair by the hardships of their lot burst upon the plain-country and plundered their Hindu enemies with all the horrors of the Jacquerie.

In time, of course, the outbreak was repressed. But the calm courage of the insurgents secured the respect of their conquerors, and the eyes of the Government were at length opened to their intolerable economical position. Redress was secured by removing the Santāls from the operation of the civil law of the plains, which was quite unsuited to their state of culture, and by placing them under the direct supervision of a body of sympathetic British officers. The success of these measures may be estimated by the notable increase in their numbers. The 30,000 emigrants who entered the Dāman-i-Koh in 1832 have now become 663,000, and including colonists who have emigrated beyond the original settlement, the tribe now numbers about two millions.

In spite of their increase in prosperity and numbers the Santāls have clung to their national customs and institutions. They are blissfully contented with life as it is, careless and improvident, completely absorbed in devotion to the soil, asking no more than that they may be left undisturbed, that their customs be respected, and their rents not unduly enhanced. Their religion is a form of Animism, and Hinduism has never taken any real hold on them. On the other hand, Christian missionary work has been strikingly successful among them. The social penalties for the offence of embracing Christianity are no less severe among them than with the castes of the plains. But the Santāl Church, which thirty years ago numbered scarcely more than three hundred, has at the present time a congregation of fifty thousand souls.

CHAPTER V

THE CASTES OF THE PLAINS

Caste: its conditions and origin. The tribal castes. The Rajput and Jat. The occupational castes. The Brahman. The Dom.

So far we have been dealing mainly with tribes, and we have seen that in the hill-country the tribe is gradually developing into the caste. When we enter the plains, we find the caste system in full vigour. It is, of course, not suggested that the geographical limits where the caste begins and the tribe ends can be accurately fixed. There are many castes in the hill-country, some formed out of immigrants from the plains, others resulting from the break-up of the tribe, and there are some tribes in the plains.

The caste, like the tribe, is a collection of families or groups of families bearing a common name. In the case of a tribe this common name does not indicate community of function. But the title of a caste usually implies that all its members follow the same occupation, as when we speak of Lohārs or blacksmiths, Mālis or gardeners, and so on. Secondly, the caste usually claims common descent from a mythical ancestor, human or divine, while the tribe sometimes traces its origin from some animal, which may be treated with respect or may possibly be regarded as its totem. Thirdly, the tribe, not the caste, generally occupies, or is supposed to occupy, a well-defined area, which is not the case with a caste, members of which are found scattered all over the country. Lastly, the strict law of endogamy does not always apply to the tribe; that is to say, its members may find wives among the members of another tribe. The caste, on the contrary, is always endogamous, and in addition it is generally divided into sections or sub-castes, each of which is endogamous. Thus in Bombay the Brahman caste numbers about a million souls, and is divided into more than two hundred of these groups, none of which permit intermarriage. Each group, again, or as it may be better called, each subordinate caste, contains a number of sections, to which the name Gotra is usually given, the members of which are bound to marry outside their section. In all cases marriage outside the group or sub-caste or within the section invariably results in expulsion.

It is not proposed to discuss at length the vexed question of the origin of caste. The subject has been discussed *ad nauseam*, and so far without much definite result. One fact is clear, that we must revise the current idea of the extreme antiquity of caste as we find it in existence. The popular view is based on a literature which was all the work of Brahmans, deeply interested in asserting the divine origin of an institution in which they are the leading members. But the sacred books of the Buddhists and Jains show the other side of the question, and from them it is clear that caste, as we now understand the term, had its origin in the Buddhist age, some six centuries before the Christian era. At that time it was, so to speak, only in the making; the strict rules prohibiting intermarriage between the groups were not in existence, and the predominance of the Brahmans was not assured.

In ancient India there were distinctions of social rank, but as might have been expected, these connoted colour, the contrast of the fair-skinned Aryan with the black, broad-nosed Dravidian. But this in no way corresponded with caste as we see it at present.

The question remains—How did this sense of distinction of race as indicated by difference of colour develop into the modern system of caste? Mr. Risley thus attempts to explain it: 'Once started in India the principle was strengthened, perpetuated, and extended to all ranks of society by the fiction that people who speak a different language, dwell in a different district, worship different gods, eat different food, observe different social customs, follow a different profession, or practise the same profession in a slightly different way, must be so unmistakably aliens by blood that intermarriage with them is a thing not to be thought of.' Mr. Risley admits that the origin of caste, from the nature of the case, must remain an insoluble problem, and 'the particular conjecture now put forward is based, first, upon the correspondence that can be traced between certain caste gradations and variations of physical type; secondly, on the development of mixed races from stocks of different colour; and, thirdly, on the influence of fiction.'

The groups which we now call castes have been since the time of their creation so greatly modified and reconstructed that it is now practically impossible to distinguish castes which may once have been tribes from others which are due to the crystallisation of occupations—trade guilds, as they may be called—or groups formed in the many ways suggested by Mr. Risley. Hence it is perhaps going too far to name, as he does, the Ahīr or cowherd, the Dom and Dusādh menials, the Gūjar cattle-breeder, the Jat husbandman, the Meo, a half-Hinduised jungle-man, and the Rajput as castes whose development from original tribes can with more or less confidence be assumed. Possibly this may be the case, but we have no real evidence of such a process of evolution. These castes are, it is true, concerned with the most primitive industries, and they are almost certainly older than castes, like those of the lapidary or jeweller, which minister to the wants of a highly civilised people.

Two of this kind of castes, which may for the sake of convenience be called 'tribal,' the Rajputs and the Jats, are of much interest and importance, and may be considered before we come to the Brahmans, a caste largely derived from specialisation of function.

The term Rajput means literally 'son of a Raja,' in the sense that they claim to be descended from a ruling race. They are found to the number of nine and a half millions throughout Northern India, and exercise sovereignty in some of the independent States of Rajputana. Some of them, like the ruling family of Udaipur, claim to possess the bluest blood in the country, and trace their pedigree back to the demi-god Rāma, whence they call themselves Children of the Sun. They assert that they represent the ancient race of Kshatriyas or warriors, and boast that their honour was never stained by giving a princess of their family in marriage to a Moghul emperor.

The status of many of the Rajput tribes settled within British territory is much lower than that of the princely families of the west. Their legends and physique indicate that in their case Aryan blood has been mixed with that of lower tribes. We have seen that jungle-folk, like Gonds and Khasas, occasionally rise to the rank of Rajputs. This has led to a gradation of rank among the septs, those on the west being closer to Rajputana, holding a rank higher than those of the more eastern districts.

The marriage law of the Rajputs deserves mention. It has received from ethnologists the name of hypergamy; that is to say, a Rajput must marry his daughter in a sept which is at least not lower than his own. This naturally leads to a scarcity of brides in the highest septs, and the influence of infanticide contributes to the same result. Hence low-caste girls are often introduced in the guise of high-born brides. In some cases the husband is the victim of deliberate fraud on the part of the matchmaker. But often the arrangement seems to be accepted as a necessary evil by the clan; and even when a man finds that he has been defrauded, the dread of scandal prevents him from giving publicity to his grievance.

The Rajputs first appear in history as rulers of

kingdoms in the valleys of the Ganges and Jumna, with their chief capitals at Delhi and Kanauj, which were overwhelmed by the Mohammedans at the close of the tenth century of our era. This destruction of the Rajput power had important results. Some of the dispersed tribesmen fled for refuge to the hills, where we have already noticed their presence. Others advanced further to the east, pushed on by the advancing Mohammedans, and settled in the broad, fat lands of Oudh and Behar, where we find their descendants heads of village communities at the present day. Another body, destined to exercise a more commanding influence on Indian politics, turned westward, and sought the arid land now called Rajputana, where they founded independent States, each the rallying point of a single sept.

In this country the Rajputs have maintained their tribal system and freedom unimpaired. They resisted the Moghul emperors, who had gained the lordship of all the remaining part of Northern India. Later on they endured grievous stress from the Mahrattas, from which they were saved by British intervention.

In a Rajput State the chief is the head of the clan by whom the country was settled. He is not a despot, but exercises a jurisdiction more or less limited over an aristocracy, the members of which are his kinsmen and connections. It is only outside their fiefs and in the capital that his authority is absolute. The land pays a rent to the ruling chief, who must of necessity be a Rajput, or to the holder of a fief under him; and in the western States, which are

Bhotiyas of Kumaun, Northern Hills (p. 49)

the most conservative of ancient tradition, practically all the soil is in Rajput hands. The chief is venerated as representing the bluest blood of the dominant clan. Succession to office goes by primogeniture, and cannot pass through females. In most cases the right of adoption has been recognised by the Imperial Government; but sometimes, when direct heirs fail, the new chief is selected by the barons from the leaders of the clan. In the final resort the British Government adjudicates on the rights of the candidates.

This is not exactly feudalism, but something resembling it. It is the only really free constitution within the Empire. While their brethren, who clung to their homes in the Ganges valley, have become heads or members of a village community, the braver spirits transplanted to the western desert a compact tribal organisation, which has displayed wonderful vitality, and bears as much promise of permanence as any institution in the East. The dry air of the desert has hardened the muscle and strengthened the chivalry of this the most interesting people in Northern India.

The life of the Rajput in the British districts is not calculated to develop the manly virtues. He preserves the tradition that his ancestors were princes, and he despises trade and industrial pursuits. Few of them attain the standard of education which fits them for civil employment. He cannot serve as a soldier of fortune, and as a result of the want of fitting occupation, dissipation and excessive use of drugs or spirits are common among them. The land is so closely cultivated that facilities for sport are much restricted, and they have lost the taste for manly exercises which harden the muscle and develop the physique. In the absence of healthier forms of amusement the Rajput often seeks to avoid ennui by carrying on a lawsuit. In a land where evidence can be bought and sold, and where advocates of the baser sort make a trade of chicanery, this usually supplies abundant excitement. If the Rajput holds a farm it is usually ill-managed, because he is too proud to follow the plough himself, and depends upon hired labour. His house is pretentious, but badly kept, and he dispenses a rude hospitality, and indulges in foolish expenditure on the occasion of marriages and deaths, which often drives him into the hands of the money-lender. At the same time his dignity of manner, his courtliness of address, and his *bonhomie* make him a pleasant companion and a favourite with the British officer.

Most competent observers of Rajputs and Jats in the south-eastern Punjab consider them to be branches of the same stock. Sir D. Ibbetson concludes that they were not the result of successive migrations. He accepts the popular native view that the Rajputs represent those members of the group who maintained the purity of their blood and a high standard of orthodox Hindu life. The Jats, failing to satisfy these requirements, have sunk to a lower level by devoting themselves to farming, by sanctioning widow-marriage, and allowing their women to work in the fields.

The Jats are a most interesting people, but their stolidity and reticence make it difficult to learn much about them. This character seems to be largely the result of environment—they have grown grave and impassive like the great white oxen which they prize so dearly. The Jat is the typical yeoman, the finest farmer in Northern India. His knowledge of crops and cattle is unrivalled, and his industry is unceasing. Every member of the family, from the old crone down to tiny children, shares in the field-work. In this he is so absorbed that the higher things of life have little interest for him. *Parcus deorŭm cultor et infrequens*—he cares little for the Brahman and his rites. The keen wit of the country-side gibes at him as a stolid boor, and such a tough customer is he when armed with his iron-bound quarter-staff that you should never be sure that he is dead till the thirteenth day of mourning has passed. But he is a fine, manly fellow, and has special interest for us because his tribe supplies some of our best Sikh sepoys.

The Sikh shares with the Gurkha and Pathān the highest reputation in our Indian army. To compare the Sikh with the Pathān, the physique of the former is perhaps superior, while the latter has more activity and endurance. The Sikh looks the finer man, and his beard, which is never trimmed, and twined up on the cheek, adds to his dignity. 'In character,' Mr. Gore remarks, 'the Sikhs are often almost bovine in their stupidity. Being all of the yeoman class and dwellers in the plains, they are full of sturdy self-respect, resolute, obedient, and always under control. Their fighting qualities are too well known to need comment, and arise, no doubt, from their stolid and steady courage and their contempt for death; but they are wanting in the initiative and dash that go to make up a perfect soldier.' He adds that 'the comparison of the Sikhs to the Germans, and the Pathāns to the French, is not altogether an ill-suited one, and socially it is easier for the English officer to mix with the former than with the latter. For the Sikhs and ourselves have a common love for games and athletics, whereas the Pathān takes no part in either, and looks upon the Sikhs and Punjabis, who appear in a semi-nude condition at these competitions, as men utterly without shame and honour.'

The character of the Jat is reflected in his religion and tribal custom. Considerably more than half the followers of the Sikh faith come from the Jats. This is a solid, unemotional creed, in which the priesthood has little power, and every one submits to a rite of baptism in perfect equality. Among the Jats we find nothing resembling the semi-feudalism of the Rajput. Though a few of their septs have a vague and ill-defined superiority over others, in reality they are on a dead level of equality.

When we pass from Rajputs and Jats to Brahmans we find not a 'tribal' caste, but one based upon community of occupation. Brahmans are generally supposed to form one homogeneous body, all of the same rank, all devoted to the study of their sacred books, and all performing the duty of priests to the castes of lower rank. All these assertions are incorrect.

In the first place there are many grades of Brahmans. Some, like the Pandit of Benares, are tall, delicately built men, with a long, finely moulded head, and intellectual expression of countenance. The gait and style of conversation of the high-bred Brahman show his consciousness of superiority to all of a lower caste. His manner has the fine courtesy and condescension of one who expects deference from his neighbours, and regards them in a half-pitying way as men who cannot reach the heights of orthodoxy and purity which he has attained. He is, of course, precise in the outward ceremonial of his faith. In fact, it is on ritual that he depends as a means of spiritual advancement, and he puts morality in the background as a matter with which he is not immediately concerned.

The village Brahman is on a lower level than the Pandit, and in many cases has obviously inherited a strain of meaner blood. He is quite unacquainted with the dialectics of which his learned brother is a master. He hardly pretends to know any Sanskrit, save a few texts, the meaning of which he does not understand. His functions include the domestic duties, those connected with birth, marriage, the casting of a horoscope, and so on. If he has a little more than ordinary learning, he performs the duties of Purohit, or family priest, to some wealthy landowner or merchant. Writing of the Punjab, though the statement applies more or less generally to Northern India, Sir D. Ibbetson well describes the common Brahman. 'Besides the Purohits themselves there is a large body of Brahmans who, so far as their priestly office is concerned, may be said to exist only to be fed. They consist of the younger members of the Purohit families, and of Brahmans who have settled as cultivators, or otherwise, in villages where they have no hereditary clients. These men are always ready to tender their services as recipients of a dinner, thus enabling the peasant to feed the desired number of Brahmans on occasions of rejoicing, as a propitiatory offering, in token of thanksgiving, for the repose of his father's spirit, and so forth. The veneration for Brahmans runs through the whole social as well as religious life of a Hindu peasant, and takes the form of either offerings or food. No child is born, named, betrothed, or married; nobody dies or is burnt; no journey is undertaken, or auspicious day selected; no house is built, no agricultural operation begun, or harvest gathered in, without Brahmans being feed and fed; a portion of all the produce of the fields is set apart for their use; they are consulted in sickness and in death; they are feasted in sorrow and in joy; and though I believe them to possess but little real influence with the people of the Punjab, a considerable portion of the wealth of the province is diverted into their useless pockets.'

Again, it is only a minority of the caste which is engaged in religious duties of any kind. They practise all the learned professions, as lawyers, land-agents, or estate-managers; as clerks in public offices or commercial houses, as orderlies or messengers to officials, in the police, or as sepoys in the few regiments which now admit them. Large numbers of them are attached to the land, as members of proprietary village communities, or as tenants, in which occupations the rule

No. 11

Blacksmiths, Chota Nagpur (p. 133)

that they must not hold the plough or allow their women to do field-work seriously checks their prosperity.

The Brahman caste is clearly composed of various elements. Some of them, probably, as Mr. Risley suggests, are descended from the bards, ministers, and family priests of the Raja in Vedic times. By degrees religious ritual became more intricate, and thus a monopoly was created in the hands of the sacred order. But the Brahmans, as we find them at present, gained recruits from other sources. One section in the Punjab seems to represent Persian priests of the sacred fire, who entered India from Persia. Others, again, and those of the lower class, were apparently the medicine-men of those Dravidians who, when they adopted Hinduism, brought their priests with them.

The mixed origin of the caste may also be inferred from their territorial divisions. Five of these, each quite isolated from the others, are found in Northern India. These are probably descended from the priests of successive bodies of Aryan emigrants.

Four sets of Brahmans are held in special disrepute. First come the Kulin Brahmans of Bengal, whose system of 'sealing' wives in the fashion of the Mormon Church has long attracted attention, and has even formed the subject of special legislation. With them, says Mr. Risley, 'matrimony became a sort of profession, and the honour of marrying a daughter to a Bhanga Kulin is said to have been so highly valued in Eastern Bengal that as soon as a boy was ten years old his friends began to discuss his marriage prospects, and before he was twenty he had become the husband of many wives of ages varying from five to fifty.' This custom, though probably less prevalent than in former times, still continues. Mr. Gait, in his last Census Report of Bengal, writes: 'The vicious system known as Kulinism, by which a Kulin contracted the marriage ceremony with an almost unlimited number of wives whom he never took to live with him, is said to have become very uncommon; but such cases still occur, and I was told of one instance where a Kulin had married nine wives.'

The other classes of disreputable Brahmans are those who officiate as temple priests; those who frequent places of pilgrimage; those who perform the funeral rites.

The contempt exhibited towards the temple priest is probably due to the fact that idol-worship, as we observe it now at the greater shrines, is comparatively modern. The non-Aryan tribes always had their rude stone fetishes; but the anthropomorphic graven image probably dates only from later Buddhist times. Idol-worship in the sacred cities, like Benares and Muttra, has assumed enormous proportions. Every street and lane has its temples, and the crudely carved, coarsely decorated images of one or other of the gods meet the passer-by almost at every step. This is the sordid aspect of Hinduism, which in its higher forms displays much that is admirable. The abundance of temples and images necessarily leads to competition between the priests of rival shrines. Gangs of touts beset the roads leading to the holy places, and cajole the pilgrim to accept the services of a particular Brahman as a guide. For a consideration he escorts the visitor to the temple which he favours, and extorts money from him at every stage of the pilgrimage. Hence comes the low repute of the temple priest, and in particular of those harpies who infest the bathing Ghāts (Pl. 8, 9).

Among these the Gayawāls of Gaya in Behar, which is the place where the funeral rites which ensure a seat in heaven to the spirits of a man's relations can most fitly be performed; the Prayāgwāls, who control the bathing at the sacred junction of the Ganges, Jumna, and Saraswati at Allahabad; and the burly Chaubēs, who rule Muttra, the holy land of Krishna, are the most licentious and exacting.

The Gayawāls have agents all over the country who induce the pious to make pilgrimages to their city. Their manner of life is idle and vicious. They stay little at home, but pass most of their time at clubs, where they amuse themselves with athletics and the performances of dancing-girls. A Gayawāl on rising goes to his club, where he spends the morning drinking or exercising his muscles. He returns home after bathing at midday for dinner, and usually remains all night at his club. The women meanwhile are occupied in preparing betel for chewing, and doing trivial home work. But cooking, the heaviest task which falls to the lot of the Hindu matron, is left to Mahratta women, who are found in large numbers at Gaya.

The Chaubēs of Muttra are a similar class. They are celebrated more for their skill in wrestling than for priestly learning. The old religious histories of the place extol their virtues in the most extravagant terms; but either the writers were prejudiced, or time has exercised a sadly deteriorating effect. 'They are now,' says Mr. Growse, 'ordinarily described by their countrymen as a low and ignorant horde of rapacious mendicants.' They may always be seen with their portly forms lolling about the sacred places, ready to bear down on the first pilgrim that approaches. In order to maintain the exclusiveness of their guild, they are very unwilling to marry an outsider. This custom results in two exceptional usages—first, marriage contracts are often made while one, or even both, of the parties most concerned are still unborn; and, secondly, little or no regard is paid to relative age, and a Chaubē, if a friend has no available daughter to bestow upon him, will agree to wait for the first granddaughter.

The Mahabrahman, or 'great' Brahman, as he is styled with a feeling of ridicule or contempt, is the funeral priest, who lives by receiving the clothes and other effects of the dead man. The theory is that the vicarious wearing and using of such things by the Brahman provide the spirit with necessaries and luxuries during its journey to the place of departed souls. Hence this priest is regarded as an uncanny person, whom it is most unlucky to meet in the early morning. In the Punjab he announces his office by riding the despised animal, the ass. When he answers to his name in a crowded court, it is ludicrous to watch how his neighbours in the press draw in their skirts and hasten to make way for him. He sits like

No. 12

Brick-making (p. 135)

a carrion crow, the people say, watching for the death of a fat banker.

The subject of funerals takes us from the Brahman, who is at the top of the Hindu social system, to the Dom, who is at the very bottom. This is a people with no written history, and little intelligible oral tradition. But they are, in a way, one of the most remarkable races in the northern plains. Their squat figures, black complexion, and specially dark, piercing eyes show that they belong to the non-Aryan race. They have been, it is fairly certain, a race of serfs, outcasts, helots for uncounted generations. Their servile condition, as Mr. Risley says, 'would of itself be sufficient to break down whatever tribal spirit they may once have possessed, and to obliterate all structural traces of their true origin.'

The tribe is very widely dispersed, and has thus become divided into groups with divergent characteristics. Thus in Behar, and in the eastern districts of the United Provinces, we find the Maghaiya Doms, who take their name from the old kingdom of Magadha, or southern Behar. They are pure nomads, wandering about in gangs, which are often, during the absence of the adult males in jail, under the leadership of a woman. They pretend to follow the usual occupations of the gipsy—the weaving of mats, basket-making, and the like. But these are only a cloak for more nefarious practices, and the nomadic Dom is above all things indisposed to undertake steady labour. When he is partly civilised and abandons his wandering life, he is sometimes employed as a town scavenger. He has the monopoly of the duties of a public executioner, and provides the fire to light the funeral pyres.

The very touch or even the view of a Dom is a source of pollution to the respectable Hindu, and so little is known of the tribe by the general public that all sorts of marvellous tales about them are believed. Thus in Bengal it is supposed that they do not cremate or bury their dead, but dismember the corpse at night, and place the fragments in a pot which they sink in the nearest river or tank. Mr. Risley conjectures that this horrid idea was suggested by the old Hindu law, which placed these outcasts under a special taboo, and compelled them to bury their dead at night.

The Dom at the Benares burning Ghāt is a most important personage. Some years ago the head of the caste used to be conveyed to the funeral of a wealthy client in his own palanquin. When the corpse arrives at the river bank the Dom supplies five logs of wood, which he lays in order on the ground as a foundation for the pyre, which is then completed with other fuel brought by the relatives of the deceased. When the pile is ready and the body placed upon it the Dom brings a wisp of lighted straw which the chief mourner applies to the wood. In Hindu belief he only can provide fire for this purpose. Accordingly at the funeral of a person of wealth and rank his insolence is in ludicrous contrast to the contempt with which he is usually received. He has now the satisfaction of refusing to perform his hateful duty until the relatives cringe before him and propitiate him with bribes. When he acts as public executioner, he is careful before he drops the platform of the gallows to make a direct appeal to the Emperor, the convicting judge, and to all and sundry concerned in the sentence which is being inflicted on the criminal. By this he imagines that he transfers the guilt of blood from his own shoulders to those who are better able to bear it than himself.

The minor industries which the partially tamed Dom performs are distributed among the subdivisions of the caste, such as the Bānsphor, or 'cane-splitter,' who makes baskets and mats, and the Dharkār, or 'ropemaker,' who works in various fibres. But these occupations are not completely specialised, and most Doms, except those of the highest class, will on occasion work as scavengers and perform other menial duties.

The Dom shows his absolute divorce from Hindu orthodoxy by his licence in the matter of food. He is even more catholic in his tastes than the jungle-man. He will eat the leavings of every caste except that of the Dhobi, or washerman, with whom for some obscure reason he has a hereditary feud. When pressed by hunger he will consume the foulest carrion. In some places he is said to draw the line at cats, dogs, beasts of prey, the monkey, the serpent, and the lizard. But he will certainly eat tiger's flesh, and practically he has no scruples about the nature of his food. Hence the orthodox Hindu, half of whose life is occupied in the cult of pots and platters, loaths and abhors him.

Another large branch of the Doms is found in the

districts of Kumaun and Garhwāl in the lower Himālayas. They are supposed to be the survival of a menial race which once extended along as far westward as Kashmir. The other wild tribes of this region, like the forest-dwelling Rajis, disclaim all connection with them. As there is no Dravidian substratum in the Punjab, we may perhaps assume that they may have sprung from captives taken in war, enslaved and degraded by some of the early Indo-Aryan settlers who occupied the lower hills. This superior race is now perhaps represented by the Khasas or Khasiyas who have been already described.

The position of this branch of the Doms is much superior to that of the nomad tribe in Behar and the adjoining districts. They are divided into various classes of artisans and labourers—weavers, brass-founders, blacksmiths, workers in bamboo, breeders of pigs and fowls, and the like. Some of them discharge the special function of acting as priests of the local gods, as sorcerers and charmers of hail-storms, for all which duties they receive doles of grain at harvest time. This, at any rate, is some evidence that they have been long attached to the soil. All over India the hedge-priest is very often an autochthon, his long residence in the land being supposed to confer upon him the knowledge of the character and peculiarities of the local gods, and to teach him the proper mode in which they may be conciliated. Thus the Doms preserve to the present day the animistic and demonistic beliefs of the aboriginal races, which the Khasiyas, who have succeeded them, temper with the worship of the village deities, the named and localised divine entities, with the occasional languid cult of the greater Hindu gods. The propitiation of the vague spirits of wood or cliff, river or lake, they are satisfied to leave in charge of their serfs.

In the Punjab, again, the Dom appears as the Dom or Dūm Mirāsi, a sort of low-class minstrel and genealogist, whose women dance and sing, but only it is said in the shelter of the zenana and in the presence of other women. The Mirāsi attends weddings and funerals, where he recites the genealogies of the wedded pair, or describes the brave acts of the dead man's ancestors. He may be seen making his progresses mounted on a rawboned steed, the tail of which is dyed in some gaudy colour, and with a pair of kettledrums strapped across its withers. He is the Autolycus of modern India, with a fund of jokes and anecdotes with which he amuses his clients. If his fees are assured his language is suave and complimentary; but if he is made to feel that he is neglected he pours out from his well-stocked memory old, half-forgotten scandals and gibes directed against the unfortunate family which he honours with his company.

We have thus considered the two extremes of rank among the people of the plains—the Brahman, Rajput, or Jat representing the aristocracy of birth and rank, the Dom an object of abhorrence. Between these lies the great mass of the agricultural, commercial, and industrial classes, whose position will be considered in the next chapter.

CHAPTER VI

THE AGRICULTURAL, COMMERCIAL, AND INDUSTRIAL CASTES OF THE PLAINS

Bhāts and Chārans. Bhuinhārs and Tagas. Khatris. Kayasths. Banyas. Halwāis. Rules of eating and drinking. Gūjars. Ahīrs. Kurmis. Mālis. Banjāras. Bhars. Thārus. Rājis. Kalwārs. Telis. Kols. Dhānuks. Dosādhs. Koris. Pāsis. Dhobis. Khatīks. Gipsy tribes—Gulgulias. Bhangis : Chamārs : Fakīrs.

THE agricultural, commercial, and industrial castes of the plains constitute a body of people whom it is all but impossible to arrange in any semblance of order. Those at the top of the scale approximate more or less to those of the highest rank, while those at the bottom merge gradually into the menial class. At the last census an attempt was made to arrange these in order of precedence. Naturally it was found impossible to adapt such a system of classification to the Empire as a whole—not a single country, but a collection of provinces the people of which differ as Scotsmen from Neapolitans in customs, language, and religion. 'One might as well,' says Mr. Risley, 'try to construct a table of social precedence for Europe, which should bring together on the same list Spanish grandees, Swiss hotel-keepers, Turkish pashas, and Stock Exchange millionaires, and should indicate

A Potter at Work (p. 135)

the precise distinction attaching to each.' The result of such an inquiry, though of little value for the Empire as a whole, is of interest when applied to a more limited area.

It may be convenient to select for this special examination the tract known as the United Provinces of Agra and Oudh, with a population of forty-eight millions and an area of one hundred and twelve thousand square miles. It contains the upper valleys of the Ganges and Jumna, an alluvial region of great fertility inhabited by a most industrious agricultural population. On the other hand, it includes a considerable tract in the lower Himālayas and the Vindhyan hills. It is thus fairly representative of the general conditions of Northern India. On the east it is identical in climate, soil, and the character of its people with the western part of Bengal; on the west no physical or ethnical boundary separates it from the Punjab.

The census classification of its population divides it into fourteen main classes. By briefly considering these we shall obtain a bird's-eye view of the caste groups into which the people are divided.

First on the list come the Brahmans, who have been already discussed. Then follow three castes allied to Brahmans, who are recognised as holding a good social position—the Bhāt, the Bhuinhār, and the Taga.

The Bhāts are the hereditary bards or panegyrists of the leading Hindu castes. The most probable explanation of their origin is that they are a mixed caste composed both of Brahmans and Rajputs, which at a very early period was appointed to attend the courts of warrior princes, where they recited in public the praises of their clients, and kept a record of their genealogies. They and their kinsmen the Chārans played an important part in the local history of Western India, Gujarat in particular. Like the herald in classical literature, they enjoyed immunity from outrage, and their readiness to sacrifice their lives by the rite known as Trāga confirmed this feeling. Hence they were used as escorts of treasure, and in that wild borderland where brigandage was a profession, convoys were saved from attack only by the certainty that the Bhāt or Chāran would commit suicide if the property entrusted to him were plundered, and that his angry ghost would haunt his assailants. This devotion to duty was the noble side of their character. But those of the baser sort adopted the custom of enforcing their demands by threat of suicide, or even by actually killing a girl or an old woman as a means of exacting blackmail. The pressure of British law has now practically put an end to acts of this kind.

The Bhuinhārs and Tagas are in quite a different position. The Bhuinhārs, or 'landholders,' are found in Behar and the adjoining country. They occupy the curious position of claiming to have been originally Brahmans, who abandoned sacerdotal functions and took to a life of agriculture. An argument against this claim is that the sections into which they are divided are not of the Brahman, but of the Rajput type. They hold a high rank among Hindus. Two great landholders, the Maharajas of Benares and Bettiah, the former the successor of the notorious Chait Singh, the opponent of Warren Hastings, belong to this caste. The uniformity of physical type among them disposes of the suggestion that they are a mixed race. The most reasonable theory is that they are a branch of one of the Indo-Aryan stocks, which colonised that part of the country in which they are found at present, and being for some reason compelled to abandon priestly duties, if they ever practised them, took to a life of fighting and farming, and organised their caste on the model of the ancient Kshatriya or warrior class. In fact, they seem to stand to the Brahman much in the same relation as the Jat in the Punjab does to the Rajput.

The Tagas of the Upper Ganges valley in the neighbourhood of Agra have similar traditions, and enjoy a status like that of the Bhuinhārs. They constitute a fine body of yeomen, somewhat in the same class as the Jats. But while the Jat is stolid in nature, and works harder than most of the peasant class, these semi-Brahmans have all the trickiness, quarrelsomeness, and distaste for hard manual labour which are found among their brethren the priests. Many of them pretend that ploughing disgraces them, and they work their land by hired servants.

In the third class, which includes the Rajputs, are placed the Khatris, who claim Rajput descent, but are more probably akin to the mercantile class. They rank high in Punjab, being priests of the Sikhs, and the great Sikh Gurus, Nanak, and Govind, who founded that faith, were Khatris by birth. Now they are chiefly occupied in trade, and much of the commerce between Central Asia, Afghanistan, and India is in their hands. They have at all times shown great administrative ability, and Todar Mal, the famous finance minister of the Emperor Akbar, came from their ranks (Pl. 14).

Next comes a very important caste, that of the Kayasths, or writers. In Bengal they hold a rank much lower than in the country further west, where their appearance and customs justify their claim to be of comparatively pure Indo-Aryan descent. They are probably a nondescript caste, developed not earlier than the seventh century B.C., when for the first time the knowledge of writing reached the people of Northern India from the Euphrates valley through the agency of Dravidian merchants of Southern India. But their claim to enjoy high social rank has been fiercely disputed, and it is undoubtedly the habit of a pushing, ambitious caste like the Kayasths to assert a higher position than is its due. They have always been notorious for pliancy of character, and for their power of adapting themselves to the varying conditions of official life. Though Hindus by religion, they readily acquired in Moghul times the speech and script of the ruling power, and became clerks in the imperial secretariat and accountants of the village communities. When the British came upon the scene they continued to perform the same duties under the new administration. The better members of the caste enjoy a high reputation for their literary acquirements, and work with credit in the Government service and in the learned professions; but the low village writer, known as the Lala, is a byword for astuteness and chicanery.

This closes the list of castes which have any pretensions to rank as descendants of the noble Aryans. They are followed by various mercantile groups, all classed generally under the name of Banya or Mahājan, 'great man,' in the sense that he has the power of the purse. They descend from the trading class of the Aryan community, and their appearance indicates their respectable origin. Some of their women are as high-bred in appearance as any in Northern India; but they are generally secluded. This idle, unhealthy course of life rapidly destroys their beauty, and a sedentary occupation and excessive indulgence in rich food make the men corpulent and unhealthy. The Marwāris, whose home is in the Marwar State of Rajputana, have an evil repute as usurers and skinflints. They are found in all the great trading cities, and much of the economic difficulties of the peasantry may be laid to their charge. Naturally the village money-lender is an unpopular person. 'He who has a Banya for a friend needs no enemy'; 'The Thug robs the stranger, the Banya his friend,' are specimens of the proverbial wisdom of the country-side. But without the Banya agriculture could not be financed, and though his rates are high the security is often indifferent, and in business matters he is often not such a shark as he is generally reputed to be. At any rate, he gets on well with the people, and they have never risen against him as they did in the Deccan in 1875, when the debtors broke into revolt, burned the bankers' books, and, if the outbreak had not been repressed, would have treated them as an anti-Semitic mob in Eastern Europe deals with the Jews.

The trading classes, by their liberal charity, are the best supporters of the Brahman, and are the chief builders of temples in our time. Many of them have adopted the faith of the Jain sectaries, a movement, like Buddhism, directed against the pretensions of the Brahman caste. But they claim to be members of the Hindu communion, and do not prohibit intermarriage with that section which has clung to the old faith.

Below this group the census places the Jats, who, probably on ethnical grounds, deserve a higher place, had not their religious indifferentism alienated from them the sympathies of orthodox Hinduism. With these is ranked the Halwāi, or confectioner, whom the Hindu, with a shrewd regard for practical convenience, places in a high grade of purity. In this way the interests of the traveller are protected. While on a journey he can eat sweetmeats prepared by them without polluting his caste, a convenient fiction providing that the milk and butter of the sacred cow preserve them from impurity.

This leads us to the all-important question of food in connection with caste. The position of the next group depends upon the question whether high-born people will or will not drink water from their hands, or eat food cooked with butter, such as pastry and sweetmeats which they have prepared. This distinction between two classes of food, which at first sight seems puzzling and even ridiculous, is based on considerations which are quite obvious to the Hindu, and clearly rest upon expediency. The line is definitely fixed between food cooked with water alone, and that in which butter forms a part. The former includes the boiled rice and pulse, and the griddle cakes of wheat or barley meal which are the Hindu's usual food. No respectable person will touch these unless they are cooked in his own kitchen, by his own hands, by his wife, or by a Brahman, and prepared under conditions which guarantee their purity. Food cooked with butter is, as we have seen, in a different category, and subject to much less stringent rules. Again, a distinction is drawn between drinking water poured into the outstretched hands from a stranger's drinking-vessel and using it out of the vessel of another. No one will drink out of a vessel which belongs to a member of another caste, unless it be of higher rank than his own, in which case the owner of the vessel would himself be polluted. It comes to this, then, that a man may drink water poured into his hands from the vessel of a respectable stranger, while to touch the vessel with his lips would cause pollution either to himself or to the owner. This concession, again, is obviously in the interest of the traveller who is obliged to drink among strangers. But as might be expected, these precise rules are often neglected, and a man is particularly anxious not to offend when the eyes of jealous caste-fellows are on him, while he omits the usual precautions when he meets a stranger to whom he is unknown.

In the list of people from the hands of some or all of whom a high-caste Hindu can accept water or sweetmeats offered in this way is included the mass of the respectable agricultural classes and the better artisans. The law of precedence is, of course, infinitely varied, and only the general result can be indicated here. Such people, if they are farmers, are generally in the rank of tenants, not landed proprietors. If they are proprietors they usually do not own a separate landed estate, but merely a small share in a joint village community. This sturdy peasant class forms the very backbone of the country. Some of them show strong marks of Dravidian descent. Others, like the Gūjar, are of a higher type.

The Gūjar forms something like a class of his own. He has some of the dignified bearing of the Jat and Rajput, and he shares with the latter his reluctance to endure hard labour in the field with plough or mattock. He is more of a grazier than a farmer. His village is a collection of ill-kept huts, his field is a picture of neglect and bad management. His object in life is to tend the herd of buffaloes which he grazes in the rank swamps along the river-banks, and he there devotes himself to the manufacture of ghi, or clarified butter. But he has other and more disreputable ways of gaining his livelihood. He is the boldest cattle thief in the country, and the dexterity with which he can drive off an ox, disguise its footmarks, and pass it on from one receiver's stall to another until it is far out of its owner's reach, is admirable in its way. Then he commences to negotiate, and the owner, who profoundly distrusts the detective ability of the native policeman, is generally only too glad to pay blackmail for the restoration of his beast. 'A Rajput,' said a Jat to Sir D. Ibbetson, 'will steal your buffalo, but he will not send his father to say he knows where it is, and will get it back for a consideration. The Gūjar will.' 'The dog one, the cat two, the Gūjar and the Rānghar (a kindred spirit) four; were it not for these four a man might sleep with his door open,' says the village moralist. In fact, the Gūjar retains much of the dormant savagery of olden times, and when the Mutiny wrecked for a time the power of the British in the Upper Ganges Doab, it was the Gūjar who took advantage of this state of misrule, burnt and looted our cantonments. But he met with condign punishment when authority was re-established.

The other agricultural members of this group are more respectable citizens than the Gūjar. The Ahīr, like him, is grazier, but as a rule he is a law-abiding person. 'It has been suggested,' writes Sir D. Ibbetson, 'and is, I believe, held by many that Jats, Gūjars, and perhaps Ahīrs also are all of one ethnic stock; and this because there is a close communion between them. It may be that they are the same in their far-distant origin. But I think they must have entered India at different times or settled in different parts, and my reason for thinking so is because they eat and smoke together. In the case of the Jat and Rajput the reason for differentiation is obvious, the latter being of higher rank than the former. But the social standing of Jats, Gūjars, and Ahīrs being pratically identical,

I do not see why they should ever have separated if they were once the same. It is, however, possible that the Jats were the camel-grazers and perhaps husbandmen, the Gūjars the cowherds of the hills, the Ahīrs the cowherds of the plains.' In early times this may have been the case, but at the present day these industries are no longer specialised, and the pastoral tribes combine the occupation of farming with the care of flocks and herds.

In the same grade are included the Kurmi, or Kunbi, and the Māli. The Kunbis are seen at their best in the Deccan, where they sometimes take the title of Mahratta, which is more respectable than that of Kunbi, because it was identified with the great national movement under the leadership of the famous Sivaji, which led to the rule of the Peshwas at Poona. This Deccan power made a bold bid for the dominion of Northern India, but they were finally defeated by Ahmad Shah at the battle of Panipat in 1761. Their southern dominions fell into the hands of the British, and are now included in the Presidency of Bombay and the Central Provinces. But they still retain the lordship of independent States, like Gwalior and Baroda.

In Northern India their origin is doubtful. They fall into two classes, one a brown, tawny-coloured people, rather slightly framed, and possessing a fair amount of good looks; the other short, sturdy, and dark complexioned. They combine the characteristics of the dark and fair people of Northern India. They are excellent cultivators, and much of the opium-growing is done by them. The Māli or gardener, who grows flowers and vegetables for Europeans, or supplies the markets of the larger towns, and the Kāchhi, who confines himself to vegetables alone, are only improved Kunbis. Their little holdings are examples of petite culture in its highest form. Every inch of ground is utilised, most carefully tilled, and liberally manured. The well is constantly at work supplying water to the successive crops of potatoes, the finer sugar-cane sold for eating, yams and onions, with the myriad varieties of potherbs, chillies, and the like, which all classes of the people use to flavour their monotonous food.

In this class have also been placed the respectable artisans, who will be described in connection with village industries.

Below these is a group of castes, whom the orthodox Hindu may touch, but from whose hands water may not be drunk. This is a miscellaneous class containing people like the Banjāras, the wandering suttlers, of whom we hear so much in the accounts of Sir A. Wellesley's campaigns in the Deccan, where they supplied his forces with food and forage. The spread of railways has now much diminished their numbers, and their caravans of pack bullocks guarded by savage dogs, their women with free gait, wearing richly embroidered robes and abundant jewellery, are now seldom seen.

With these are ranked that remarkable race, the Bhars. They are found chiefly in Behar, Oudh, and those districts of the United Provinces which lie south of the river Jumna. They are of Dravidian blood, but their traditions seem to justify the belief that they were once a ruling race in the plains. Many old forts and reservoirs are attributed to them. Now they have sunk into the class of small cultivators, day-labourers, and ploughmen, and rank with the lower castes. In Oudh they are the pioneers of agriculture, clearing the jungle, which, when ready for the plough, they abandon to be occupied by the more settled castes (Pl. 18).

Like them are the Thārus, a mixed tribe with some Mongolian and some Dravidian blood, who occupy the malarious Terai at the foot of the lower Himālayas. It was at one time supposed that they were malaria-proof, but as a matter of fact they suffer terribly from the fevers which abound in that region. They make their living by hunting and fishing, rearing herds of cows and buffaloes, keeping pigs, fowls, and goats, and practising a rude form of husbandry. This shy, secluded people, who have little intercourse with the castes of the plains, are haunted by the terrors of the jungle in which they make their home. When darkness settles on their villages every door is barred against the bogies which lurk in the trees, or the spirits of the dead which wander round their houses demanding food and shelter. Only the terrible cry of 'Fire' will cause them to open their huts at night, and even in the daytime no Thāru will venture along a jungle path without casting a leaf, branch, or twig on the pile of rude stones which forms the shrine of Bansapti Ma, the dread mother-goddess of the forest. The plain-dwellers dread them, and suppose them to be skilled in witchcraft and sorcery. The

A NAKED HINDU FAKĪR, HARDWAR (p. 122)

women, in particular, are supposed to possess the Evil Eye, and this in its most virulent form causes the victim to waste away and die, while a less dangerous glance causes only fever. One art which they have acquired in their jungle life is that of capturing and taming wild elephants, and whenever a Khedda, or enclosure, is erected to surround a herd, the most dangerous part of the work is entrusted to the Thārus.

The condition of the Rājis, a forest tribe which occupies the lower Himālayas westward of the Thāru country, is even lower. They live almost altogether on the produce of their jungles, and their only industry is that of making rude wooden bowls, which they barter with the people of the plains for scraps of coarse cloth and grain. Food obtained in this way they store with roots and other edibles of the kind in caves, or hang it to the branches of trees for use in time of need. They are thus a little superior to the wild tribes of the Nilgiri hills, who make no provision for the future, eat their coarse food when it is abundant, and starve in those seasons when they can find nothing eatable in their forests.

With these people have been ranked two classes of manufacturers whose business gives them a low place in the social scale—the Kalwār (Pl. 25), who distils a crude spirituous liquor from the petals of the Mohwa tree, or from crude sugar; and the Teli, or oilman, who grinds the seeds of mustard or sesamum, and prepares the oil which is used for cooking and illumination. Below these comes the Kol or Baiswār (Pl. 17), one of the Dravidian tribes of the Vindhyas, who ranks with the Bhīl, Gond, or Oraon, and stands higher than the menials of the plains.

This brings us to the last two groups in the social scale—first, those whom no good Hindu will touch, but who are free from that foulest stain of uncleanness, the eating of beef; secondly, the lowest menials of all, who will eat beef, carrion, or vermin.

In the first class are some of the menial cultivating castes, such as the Dhānuk, Dosādh, Kori, and Pāsi. These are Dravidians almost of the full blood, who have sunk to the level of serfs and menials. The Dhānuk works as a village watchman, plays the drum at Hindu weddings, and his wife is the village midwife, a profession which the Hindu regards as most impure. The Dosādh is in much the same rank, and is usually a landless labourer, the most miserable, depressed class in the northern plains. Akin to him is the Pāsi, who are found in considerable numbers in Oudh. His ostensible business is tapping the toddy palm and collecting the liquor. But he also does field-work, and though his predatory habits have now been checked, he and members of castes in the same social rank supply a considerable proportion of the criminal classes. With them are ranked two classes of workmen, whose occupation is considered degrading—the Dhobi, or washerman, because he deals with foul linen and uses that despised beast, the ass; and the Khatīk, who is a goat-butcher and deals in vegetables and fruit.

Intermediate between those people and the foulest menials come the many Gipsy tribes, who are in some ways perhaps the most interesting people of the plains.

Their occupations and mode of life will be considered in the next chapter. They are, as a rule, indifferent to the morals of their women, with the result that they form a very mixed race, some showing the fairer skin and finer features of the higher castes; others the black skin and coarse noses of the Dravidian. One of the lowest types of them is that of the Gulgulias of Chota Nagpur, who live in a precarious way by snaring squirrels and monkeys, and gleaning the scanty ears of corn which the careful farmer leaves in his field. They say that they are descended from a squirrel ancestor, but the relationship does not prevent them from stabbing the animal with a long spear, an art in which they have attained wonderful dexterity. Allied to these is the horde of mongrel castes which make their living by rope-dancing, sleight of hand, exhibiting tame bears or monkeys, ways of life which are usually combined with other practices more or less disgraceful or nefarious (Pl. 21).

Lowest of all is the group which includes the Bhangi, or sweeper, and the Dom scavenger, who has been already described. The Bhangi caste, with its various groups, is a very interesting subject of study. It must not be supposed that because they have adopted a degrading occupation and are looked on with scorn by those who practise what are assumed to be cleanlier modes of livelihood, that the sweepers are in their own opinion outcasts and that they are without a caste organisation of their own. On the contrary, they have their own tribal council, which is constituted in a peculiarly elaborate way, and they rigidly enforce their own code of caste etiquette and morals. The services of such people are so essential to the welfare of the community that they are quite conscious of their own importance, and any interference with their rights and privileges ends in a general strike, which is most inconvenient to the officers who are responsible for the sanitation of the cities and larger towns.

Slightly superior to these people is the Chamār, or currier, who is a recognised village menial, receiving as perquisite the hides of dead cattle, which he tans. In return he is bound to supply shoes and other leather articles, such as the skin bag with which water is hauled up from the well to water the fields. His calling is naturally most offensive to the pious Hindu, and he is generally obliged to live in a hamlet apart from the houses of the respectable residents, and here he keeps that foul beast, the pig, whose presence in their neighbourhood Mohammedans deem most offensive. His wife acts as the midwife, and is naturally impure. These varied occupations account for the contempt with which he is regarded by the higher classes. 'The worthy die and the worthless live because the Chamār drinks from the holy Ganges' is a rural saying which represents popular feeling. At the same time, the Chamārs, who number no less than eleven millions, practically all resident in Northern India, form a most valuable element in the population, supplying excellent labourers and hard-working drudges, who endure much of the rough toil of field-work.

In this sketch of the gradation of the people no reference has been made to Fakīrs or mendicants, because they are not an ethnical group. In the three great provinces—the Punjab, the United Provinces, and Bengal—they number considerably more than a million, and the burden of supporting this horde of useless vagrants falls heavily upon the industrious castes. Besides these are the non-religious persons who live by alms. No peasantry in the world with equally scanty resources are more charitable than the Hindus, and even at the meanest hut the beggar's demand for a little cake or a handful of grain is never disregarded. In spite, therefore, of the general poverty of the lower classes of the village population, no provision for the support of the indigent, like the English poor-law, is needed. It is only when the rains fail that the liberality of the peasant requires to be supplemented by relief works organised by the State.

There are, of course, distinctions to be drawn between the learned ascetic who devotes himself to a religious life, and the sturdy vagrant who is as much a pest to honest men as is the English tramp. The high-class ascetic, if not a profitable member of the community, is a respectable man. He is often a Brahman, Rajput, or merchant, who follows the ideal set out in the sacred books in secluding himself from social life, and devoting himself to religious meditation. On the other hand, as the Fakīr group is in a great measure free from the bonds of caste, it offers a refuge to the lazy and immoral members of the community, who have been expelled from their own caste, or desire to shirk the moral rules which the brethren enforce. The mendicant Vaishnavas of Bengal supply an example of a so-called religious profession degraded by debauchery and self-indulgence (Pl. 7, 10).

Islam, also, has many groups of Fakīrs, diverse in character and reputation as those of the Hindus. Some of the Mohammedan Pīrs are persons of respectability, who are placed in charge of mosques, cemeteries, and tombs of saints or martyrs. Lower than these is the class which lives on the credulity of pilgrims, professing to work cures on hysterical patients by expelling the Jinn, or demon, which besets them, or pretending to secure the blessing of sons to the childless. Still lower are the Beshara; that is, those who, while professing the faith of the Prophet, have no definite creed or rules of life.

It is among this lower order of so-called ascetics, Hindu or Mohammedan, that fanaticism and bigotry find a congenial soil. They naturally abhor their alien rulers, who class them as impostors, and whom they in turn regard as heretics. Whenever the political sky is clouded, whenever the cry is raised that the faith is in danger because some fanatic has defiled a Hindu temple with the blood of a cow, or another bigot has flung a pig into a mosque, the inspiration of such outrages can often be traced back to the wild denunciations of some half-witted friar, who promotes religious ecstasy by the use of intoxicating drugs.

Want of space forbids the attempt to describe the social grouping of the Mohammedans. It is sufficient to say that, unlike the Hindus, they are not bound by the rules of ceremonial purity or by restrictions in the matter of food and drink. Under the democratic constitution of Islam theoretically all men are equal, and the only gradation of rank which should be recognised is based on purity of blood. The higher class which claims descent from the Prophet, or from some of his followers, consider themselves superior to those sprung from Hindu converts. But these latter have brought with them some of the rules of caste, and many of the inferior agricultural and artisan groups marry only among themselves, and are practically castes organised after the fashion of the Hindus.

CHAPTER VII

THE VILLAGE AND ITS INDUSTRIES: THE CRIMINAL AND VAGRANT TRIBES

The village craftsmen. Agriculture. Changes of occupation. The Jeweller. Other workers in metals. Carpenters: blacksmiths: potters: weavers: dyers: tailors: washermen. Vagrant, criminal, Gipsy tribes. Ods: Chāngars: Bāwarias: Aheris: Sānsis: Meos: Nats: Kanjars. Survival and decay of village industries.

THE most primitive village life is found in the hilly country which flanks the plains. In the southern jungles, Bhīls, Gonds, or Oraons occupy an ill-defined tract of forest land. As cultivation is scattered and intermittent, the plan of the hamlet is straggling, and the huts are placed in positions convenient for the sowing and watching of the fields. Beyond these lies an area of waste, which has as yet acquired no economic value to the small body of settlers who hunt or collect wild produce within its limits. In the Himālayas the conditions are similar, and the villages are planted in narrow valleys, where the adjoining slopes give room for terrace cultivation, and a sufficient water-supply is available. The people are so law-abiding and so unfamiliar with the stress of war and rapine which have so often desolated the plains, that they have never been accustomed to combine for purposes of self-defence, or to construct the massive villages, each a little fortress in itself, which we see in the western plains.

In the most fertile districts of the plains, with which we are now specially concerned, the condition is different. All the land has been long ago occupied and demarcated, and nothing remains of the jungle with which the country was once covered except a small patch of waste land attached to each village, which supplies commonage, grazing, and fuel to the residents. The size of the village varies according to local circumstances. Where the soil is fertile and the population numerous, we meet these little settlements at every half-mile or so. The purely agricultural village differs from that in which the people, besides farming, carry on some trade or industry. In the former the houses are limited to the accommodation of the families who can conveniently cultivate the land accessible from the site. When this limit is exceeded a process of fission follows, a hamlet is founded, which gradually separates from the parent village, and sets up on its own account. In the larger villages some trade or industry is carried on, and a bazaar is founded which supplies the wants of the people. These smaller villages are the creation of an age of peace. In the Bengal delta the village is merely a collection of isolated houses. Further west the closely massed houses, with their high walls of brick or clay, become a fortress, a refuge against hostile attack.

No single family by its unaided labours could found a settlement of this kind. Before farming is started the jungle must be felled to expel malaria and wild beasts, and in the drier districts wells and tanks must be dug by the co-operation of a large body of settlers. Hence these villages are tribal, and though some of the lands may have been alienated, they still preserve traces of their tribal origin.

Captain Luard, writing of Central India, thus describes the two classes of village. In that of the jungle-folk, 'instead of a cluster of red-tiled cottages, we find a small collection of mud and wattle huts only built perhaps within the last week, and which will be at once abandoned by its timid owners if they are seized with any fear of molestation or sickness. Permanency does not distinguish these villages, at any rate as regards site, though a similar collection of huts will be erected elsewhere, leaving the total number of occupied villages as it was.' In the settled tracts 'the average village community has not changed materially from the old-fashioned, stereotyped body of people, including just the necessary classes to make it self-supplying in every economic aspect. The agricultural Kurmi, the Gadaria herdsman, the village priest of Brahman caste, the local Bania who supplies food and lends money, the Chamār who skins the dead animals, the menial Balai who runs messages and acts as watchmen, form the ordinary members of a village community.'

In the plains this primitive arrangement has in a great measure passed away. Theoretically the village consists of a body of clansmen who divide the arable land and share jointly in the cultivable waste. They

A HINDU FAKĪR LYING ON A BED OF NAILS (p. 122)

should have a head-man to control their affairs, and collect the rent owed to the State. But our system encourages the growth of private rights of property, and the old village system is gradually falling into decay. There are still, however, certain artisans attached to the village who receive doles at harvest in return for their services. The number and duties of these menials differ in various parts. Thus to the east of the United Provinces the servants entitled to these doles are the barber, who besides his ordinary duties appears at weddings, and often acts as a match-maker; the washerman; the carpenter and blacksmith, who supply the wood and iron work for the simple implements and furniture; the cowherd, who grazes the village flocks. Doles on a smaller scale are granted to the astrologer, who fixes the auspicious times for field-work; to the Kahār, or bearer, who attends on strangers; to the Kumhār, or potter, who provides earthenware; to the exorcist, who keeps the place clear of evil spirits. In the hill villages an important officer is the charmer, who protects the crops from hail. When we reach the Punjab the Mohammedan atmosphere shows itself in the list of village servants, including, besides some of those above named, the gravedigger, the Mirāsi or genealogist, and the Imām or priest of the village mosque.

Of village industries the most important of all is agriculture, which supports between sixty and seventy per cent. of the population. It is this fact which renders famine or even scarcity so destructive. But there is no clear line of distinction between agriculture and other industries. Each of the village craftsmen has a little plot, which he cultivates in his leisure hours, and which thus helps to support his family. The statistics do not fully illustrate this condition of things, because even when a man derives his support mainly or largely from some other employment, he is wont to return at the census his traditional trade industry. Thus the man whose loom is quite insufficient to provide food for his family will call himself a weaver, although much of his earnings may be derived from cultivation or day labour.

In the Punjab there is no general movement in progress by which the occupational castes are abandoning their traditional employments. Among the lower Hindu castes a man engaged in an occupation which renders him contemptible in the eyes of his neighbours, such as the currier or sweeper, when he aspires to rise in social rank, adopts Islam, and starts one of the minor industries which require little training. Thence the progress to a higher life is easy. It is tersely described in the common saying: 'The year before last I was a butcher; last year a Sheikh (or respectable Mohammedan); this year, if prices rise, I will become a Sayyid (or descendant of the Prophet).' On the other hand, in Bengal, where industrialism has made more active progress, many of the functional castes are abandoning their old industries. The Ahīr, for instance, is in theory a dairyman; but in Behar four-fifths of them are cultivators. The Chamār should work in leather, but in Behar hardly one in fifteen carries on this business.

Hence village industries, like everything else in the Indian social world, group themselves according to the supposed purity of the occupation.

The highest in the list are perhaps those connected with metals. The Sonār, or goldsmith, is one of the leading workmen. Jewellery, worn partly for purposes of ornament, partly as a talisman, forms a convenient reserve of easily realisable capital, and when need arises the precious metals are promptly melted down and sold. The function of the jeweller thus merges in that of the money-lender, and he is often suspected of acting as a 'fence,' and placing his melting-pot at the disposal of the burglar. The ordinary native has a profound suspicion of him, and it is interesting to watch a rustic bringing a piece of gold to have it worked up into a nose-ring for his wife. On such an occasion he takes care to bring with him sundry trusty friends, who watch the craftsman with distrustful eyes lest he may purloin part of the metal, or substitute bad material for good. 'The jewel belongs to the wearer, but the gold remains with the Sonār'; 'A goldsmith will steal a scrap of his mother's nose-ring,' are popular sayings which illustrate his character. The village Sonār confines himself to the simple traditional patterns which suit the taste of his customers. The basis of the design is generally the fruit, leaf, or blossom of some holy tree, thus showing that the jewel was a talisman before it became an ornament.

The workers in brass, copper, and bell-metal hold a position nearly as respectable as that of the Sonār. But these industries, owing to the increase of travelling, tend to concentrate themselves in the towns, and particularly at places of pilgrimage, where the visitor buys as a memento of his visit a lotah or water-pot, and a small brass image of the deity who is specially reverenced there. Copper, except for utensils used in the service of the gods, has gone out of use among Hindus. But Mohammedans prefer cooking- and water-pots made of that metal. Among Hindus the use of brass or bell-metal for household utensils is universal, and since each member of a well-regulated family should possess at least a water-vessel of his own, the number of such articles made and sold is enormous. They take the place of much of our furniture in the house of the peasant, and, as in the case of jewels, he invests much of his surplus cash in purchasing them, because their value is easily realised at the village pawnshop or at the factory of the brazier. Closely connected with this is the important industry of making the brass, bell-metal, or pewter bangles or anklets which the women of the lower orders commonly wear. The weight of these is so enormous that in Western Bengal they give a shuffling gait to the wearer.

The Lohār, or smith, is in a grade much lower than that of these craftsmen. He works in a metal which is uncanny because it has only quite recently replaced flint, and 'cauld iron' is believed to possess sundry mystic virtues. The blacksmith thus inherits some of the dread or contempt which attached to the first man who worked in this novel material. In the Punjab his status is low even for a menial, and he is regarded as so impure that Jats and other people of the same standing, though they do not consider him an outcast like the scavenger, will have no communion with him. He is usually remunerated by a dole of grain levied on each plough belonging to his constituents, in return for which he makes or repairs ploughshares, mattocks, weeding-spuds, and other rude implements used by the farmer. Formerly most of the iron used was of native manufacture, such as is still made in small quantities by the Agarias, a secluded jungle tribe in Chota Nagpur and the immediate neighbourhood, who smelt the ore dug from their hills with charcoal derived from the scrub jungle with which their country is covered. But this has now been almost altogether replaced by iron imported from abroad, and with it come manufactured tools and pots which still further interfere with the poor earnings of the Lohār.

The Lohār (Pl. 19) as we meet him in the plains is clearly of non-Aryan descent, intermingled with a strain of better blood. But in Central India and in parts of the Punjab we meet a race of people known as Gadiya Lohārs, that is to say, 'smiths accompanied by carts,' and Ghisāras, or 'knife-grinders.' They are short, wiry men, with black skins, high cheek-bones, and thick lips, whose original home is believed to be the Deccan or Southern India. They are a migratory people, moving about with their wives and families, attended by carts in which they convey their materials and tools. They remind us in some ways of the European Gipsy tinker. They are better workmen than the village Lohār, and do fine work which he declines to undertake.

The village carpenter (Pl. 23), the Tarkhān of the Punjab and the Barhāi of the United Provinces, enjoys much the same rank as the Lohār. In fact, the two classes are very closely connected, and each sometimes does the work of the other. The carpenter is also a village menial, and his work for his constituents lasts during seven months of the year, from the time when the first sowings start about the month of June till the spring, when the winter crops are ripe. During this period he is steadily employed in making and mending carts, well-gear, farm implements, cotton-gins, and sugar-mills, for which he receives in Oudh about 20 lb. of grain from the owner of each village plough at both harvests, that of the autumn and that of the spring. During the rest of the year he works on his own account, and if he be a superior artificer, employs his time in making the wooden pans in which the housewife kneads her dough, or in turning what are called 'Benares' toys, which he paints in gaudy colours by rubbing sticks of lac or sealing-wax of varied tints on the wood as it revolves in the lathe, the friction melting a tiny quantity which adheres to the surface of the sphere. But here, too, the occupation is becoming specialised—the better-class workman migrating to the towns and doing superior work, such as wood-carving or coach-building. In many villages he combines the functions of carpenter and blacksmith, and is the general handyman. It may be noted that he uses his toes as well as his hands to hold the wood, and that he works the saw in a way the reverse of the European craftsman, and hence its teeth are cut in the opposite direction.

These are the respectable craftsmen attached to the community. Those of the second grade are much lower in rank. An example of these is the Kumhār, or potter (Pl. 21), who is an indispensable servant, because his wares are so fragile and so liable to pollution that they must be constantly replaced. In an old village the mound on which it stands is little more than a mass of potsherds. The household utensils which he provides range from the Ghara, or globular water-jar, which the women poise so gracefully on their heads as they fetch water from the well or tank, to the great Nānd in which chaff is served to the oxen, or the still larger granary in which the corn is placed to protect it from weevils and mice. In those districts where irrigation is done by means of the Persian wheel, he has to find a constant supply of the little jars which are attached to its rim, and are constantly broken. Sometimes he makes bricks (Pl. 20), which are generally merely dried in the sun. It is only for a temple or large house, like that of the landlord or the money-lender, that burnt brick is used. The same is the case with tiles, which in the better houses replace the thatch of straw or reed. But they must be carefully guarded with thorns to keep off the monkeys which scamper over the roofs.

The potter works in the open air, and as he must have dry weather to harden his pots before they are fired, he is out of work in the rainy season, when he attends to his field or finds work as a day-labourer. Though the business of making pots is itself cleanly, he is obliged to collect all sorts of refuse to fire his kiln, and for this purpose he employs the despised ass—two disqualifications which put him outside the pale of respectable society. The pious Hindu explains by a fiction the low opinion he holds regarding him. He is, he says, a butcher, because he cuts the throats of his pots as he takes them from his wheel. 'Had he cut human throats,' grimly remarked Dr. Buchanan Hamilton,' he would have attained a higher station.' The common clay pot is such a perishable article that it is little valued, and caste prejudices prevent the use of the finer kinds of pottery, Hence no artistic industry, like that of china, has flourished in India, although kaolin and other suitable kinds of clay are in some places abundant.

Weaving is by far the most important of the village industries. Even in spite of the enormous imports of cotton fabrics from Lancashire, America, and from the mills at Bombay, Cawnpore, and elsewhere, it is estimated that sixty per cent. of the cloth used is produced at home. Much of the village-made cloth is coarse, but it is genuine, and not loaded with clay and other adulterants like some of the mill-made fabrics. The thread which the weaver uses is often spun locally by women, in connection with whose industries reference will be made to it. Much, however, is now purchased from the mills. This industry permits much co-operation of labour. The arranging of the warp is done in the open air under a shady tree. The head of the family superintends the women and children, who walk up and down the long rows of stretchers and combine the varied coloured threads from a revolving reel. When this operation is done, a thin bamboo is placed between the two layers of warp to preserve the arrangement, and the whole is then rolled up and starched. The weaver himself then spreads out the warp on stretchers, and rubs it up and down with a peculiar brush, something like an English carpet-broom without the long handle. This smooths the yarn, causing the loose ends to adhere to the main thread. At the same time opportunity is taken to mend any broken threads by twisting the ends together.

The loom is of the ordinary primitive type, closely resembling the machine which is used to this day in the Hebrides (Pl. 22). The work is done indoors, and though sufficient air enters through the chinks and crevices in the walls and roof of the crazy shed which forms the factory, the light is bad and the position of the workman cramped and unhealthy. Hence the physique of the Jolāha, or weaver, is generally inferior to that of other village craftsmen, and he is the butt of his neighbours who lead a healthy life out of doors, and understand crops and cattle of which he is ignorant. 'The goat of the Jolāha, and given to butting!' 'The ass eats the crop and the Jolāha gets thrashed!'; 'The weaver's arrow!' And yet in spite of his cowardice and boorishness he is a quarrelsome fellow; 'Eight weavers quarrelling over nine pipes!'

The other village workmen concerned with cloth are

the dyer, the calico-printer, the tailor, the washerman. The industries of the dyer and printer under the stress of foreign competition are in a state of depression; but some encouragement has been given to the latter by the demand among Anglo-Indians for curtains and floorcloths. The shawl industry of Kashmir gave a start to the finer styles of dyeing, and the splendour of native courts at Agra, Delhi, or Lucknow, fostered a trade in gaudy fabrics which has not survived the British practical rule. With the appearance some forty years ago of European chemical dyes, the use of the native vegetable pigments ceased, and the same change has exercised a ruinous effect on the carpet industry. As regards cloth, the imitation of European fashions among the higher classes has led to the substitution of the shawl by English broad-cloth and tweed. The trade in stamping cotton fabrics seems to have originated in the old capital of Kanauj, and it still survives in the neighbouring city of Farrukhabad. The prosperity of the trade depends entirely on fashion, and it is uncertain whether the progress recently made will be permanent.

The Darzi, or tailor, is hardly a regular village craftsman. The trade has never been important among the Hindus, who do not, as a rule, wear tailor-made clothes. It is only in places where the Mohammedan or English style of dress prevails that the business flourishes. Of this higher form of the trade there are various kinds, such as the making of the elaborate turbans worn by office clerks and domestic servants, the gaudy embroidered caps which the young man of fashion prefers, and the making of tents, an important industry in a

A Mohammedan Fakīr (p. 122)

country where practically all officials live under canvas during the cold season. Hence the trade of the Darzi is precarious. As the common proverb expresses it—'His needle is now in embroidery, now in canvas.' The craft of the tailor is not one of the specialised industries, and is practised by people of many castes and of different religions.

The Dhobi, or washerman, who deals in foul linen, and specially that used by persons in a state of taboo, such as women at parturition, is naturally a person of no estimation. He is not an essential member of a Hindu village community, because nearly every man, as he takes his morning bath, washes and wrings out his own loin-cloth, and his wife seldom washes the single sheet which forms her only dress. The Dhobi's methods are even cruder than those of his western sister. His mode of washing a shirt is to soap it, and then to pound it on a stone until the dirt disappears from what remains of the garment. 'His son,' says the rustic jibe, 'may be as lovely as the moon, but he bangs your clothes about till they are nought but rags'; 'The Dhobi's to-morrow is next week'; 'When many Dhobis compete, then only does soap reach the wash.'

So far we have been dealing with the settled village castes of farmers and artisans. Outside these lies a group of what may be called 'unsettled tribes,' bodies of nomads or vagrants, who practise various elementary industries, but who gain their livelihood principally by theft or other nefarious means. These people are generally denominated the Vagrant and Criminal Tribes. With these are usually grouped those of

Gipsy affinities, and indeed it is difficult to draw the line between them. They all lead a more or less wandering life, and they can only be vaguely distinguished into two classes: first, the vagrant, criminal, and hunting tribes; secondly, those who earn their living by performances of many kinds, such as exhibiting tame bears or monkeys, singing, dancing, and the like (Pl. 31). These people are singularly interesting, not only because they seem to be the ethnical representatives of the pre-Aryan races, but because they retain in an age of civilisation the ways of life which characterise a very primitive stage of culture.

Those in Bengal and the United Provinces are probably almost pure Dravidians, the colour of the face dark, the nose and jaw coarsely moulded, the eyes black and bright, all easily to be distinguished from those castes in whose veins runs a larger amount of Aryan blood. The origin of those in the Punjab is less certain, because the Dravidian element never seems to have entered that province. Many of them are probably the descendants of slaves or serfs who came in the train of the earlier settlers.

In the Punjab they may be roughly divided into three groups—the first including the Ods and Chāngars, who have a definite occupation, but no fixed dwelling-place; secondly, the Bāwaria, the Thori, the Sānsi, the Pakhiwāra, the Jhabel, the Kehal, and the Gagra, who are hunters and fishermen, living a more or less vagrant life in the jungles and on the river-banks. They are often, though not invariably, addicted to crime. Thirdly, the Mīnas and the Hārnis, who form partially nomadic criminal gangs, the women and children usually occupying fixed dwellings, while the men travel about in search of opportunities for theft.

The Ods form a tribe of wandering navvies, of whom representatives have been traced as far south as Hyderabad in the Deccan. They travel about with their families in search of work on railways and canals, and settle down in temporary huts wherever their services are required. The men do the hard labour of digging, the women carry the earth in baskets, and load the panniers of the donkeys which they always keep in their camps, and the children drive the animals to the spoil-bank. They eat anything and everything, and preserve the curious habit of always wearing a single woollen garment. This custom they explain by a legend that the founder of their tribe vowed never to drink twice out of the same well. So he dug a fresh one every day; but once he dug down and down, and never came up again. As a sign of mourning for him they dress in wool. They marry in the Hindu fashion, and bury their dead like Mohammedans. The standard religions are, in fact, only a thin veneer on the Animism, which is their real belief. In the Punjab, though classed as a vagrant tribe, they are singularly free from crime. The Chāngars are peculiar to the Punjab, and their name seems to mean 'sifters of grain.' This and reaping are their chief occupations. From some fancied similarity of name they have been, without any good reason, identified with the Zingari Gipsies of Europe.

Passing to the second group, the Bāwarias, whose original home is in the Punjab, whence a few have passed eastwards into the United Provinces, seem to derive their name from the peculiar form of snare which they use in catching game. They set a line of these nooses along a track in the jungle, on each side of which they plant scarecrows, and drive the deer or other animals into the traps. They make a speciality of catching lizards by watching when one of these animals enters its shallow hole. They then strike the place where the animal is supposed to lie with a heavy spiked mallet. Another method which they are said to employ has unfortunately not been verified by any European observer. A wisp of grass is tied to a long, elastic stick, which is thrust into the animal's hole. The lizard, believing it to be a snake, comes out tail foremost, as the native authorities say, 'that he may not see his executioner.' The sportsman promptly seizes his tail and drags him out before he has time to learn his mistake.

The Aheri, or Thori, the former possibly identical with the Aheria of the United Provinces, is primarily a hunter and fowler. In the Punjab he is often a vagrant, but sometimes becomes partially tamed, and settles in a village where he finds employment. He catches and eats all kinds of animals, pure and impure, and works in reeds and grass. He makes the leaf platters which Hindus use at caste or tribal feasts, or on a journey when the usual metal vessels are not at hand. But his chief business is highway robbery.

The Sānsi, Habura, or Bhātu is a criminal of even a more dangerous type. They wander about in gangs, and make attacks by night upon a merchant's caravan or a wedding-party, the onslaught beginning with a shower of stones, followed up by blows from the heavy quarter-staves with which they are armed. Their religion consists mainly in rude rites of propitiating the mother-goddess, and the consecration of the weapons or torches which they use. The first wife is married under caste rules, but they keep as many concubines as they can afford, and the union with these is accompanied by no rite save the approval of the tribal council. Like all these vagrant tribes, they have an elaborate argot which is not intelligible to strangers. Many efforts have been made to reform these people—by segregation of the adults in industrial settlements, by establishing reformatories for the younger members. But migratory and predatory habits are a part of their nature, and sooner or later they revert to their old, disreputable ways of life.

Another important branch of these robber tribes is that of the Meos, or Mīnas, whose headquarters are in the wilder parts of Rajputana, with branches in the Punjab, Central India, and the United Provinces. They are a mixed race, in whom Dravidian blood predominates. 'The tribe,' writes Sir A. Lyall, 'appears to be composed of various elements. With them a captured woman is solemnly admitted by a form of adoption into one circle of affinity, in order that she may be lawfully married into another, a fiction which looks very like the survival of a custom that may once have been universal among all classes at a more elastic stage of their growth; for it enables the circles of affinity within a tribe to increase and multiply their numbers without a break, while at the same time it satisfies the conditions of lawful intermarriage.' In the Alwar State they form a large agricultural tribe settled in villages, and leading a fairly respectable life. Their chief faults are a lack of industry and patience, and they compel their women to do most of the field-work. But in Central India Sir J. Malcolm described them as 'most desperate rogues.' 'Though they are stigmatised,' he goes on to say, 'as robbers and assassins, they are admitted to be faithful and courageous guards and servants. Their chiefs invariably took the lead in robberies on a large scale.' In the Punjab they are the boldest of the criminal classes, leaving their villages in gangs which sometimes remain absent for a year at a time. They have agents and 'fences' in all the larger cities of Central and Southern India, and commit robberies throughout the Deccan. After a successful foray they offer a tithe of the plunder to their guardian goddess, Kali Devi.

The so-called Gipsy tribes differ little in appearance from these criminal groups. They have the short stature, black skin, and keen black eyes of the Dravidian; but the face has become finer and the nose more shapely by intermixture with higher races. They can hardly be ranked as distinct tribes, because they permit outsiders to enter their community, and those who are acrobats often kidnap children, and train them to follow their profession. The typical name for such people is Nat, 'dancer,' or Bāzigar, 'performer,' in Northern India, while in the Deccan the Kolhātis are probably a branch of the same race, or rather a mongrel group associated in the same way of life. Among most of these people the girls, on coming of age, are given the alternative of marrying within the tribe and leading what is for them a respectable life, or of becoming acrobats and prostitutes. These are their chief occupations, but to them they add various Gipsy industries—making boxes out of hide, horn combs, little baskets of grass or reed. Tattooing of girls is an art specialised by the Nats. The operator, generally a woman, incises the design on the skin with a bundle of English needles bound round with thread, and rubs indigo into the wound. Besides tattooing, the women practise the arts of cupping, dentistry in the form of pretending to extract worms from carious teeth, and palmistry. They wander through the villages with a quantity of simples, herbs, and dried skins of birds and the smaller animals which are used in compounding charms and preparing amulets. They make a speciality of prescribing for the ailments of women. Though the women who perform as acrobats are dissolute, those who have adopted a married life are so careful in their conduct that if they do not return from these expeditions before the first cry of the jackal is heard in the evening, they are subject to severe punishment, and an intrigue with a stranger to the tribe involves immediate expulsion.

The Kanjars form a tribe of the same class and are found chiefly in the Punjab and in the United Provinces. In his natural state the Kanjar is a forest-dweller, living on any fruits or roots which his women can collect.

He is clever in trapping birds, squirrels, and any kind of vermin which comes in his way, all of which he eats without discrimination. As he becomes tamer he keeps in touch with a village where he can procure necessaries by barter. At this stage he begins to practise divers rude industries, making baskets, fans, rattles to amuse children, ropes of jungle fibres, skins with which drums are covered, platters for Hindus, mats, and other things of the same kind. He has a monopoly of making the reed brushes which the weaver uses to clean the yarn, and of collecting the fragrant grass roots which are woven into screens to cool houses in the hot weather. His weapons are the pellet-bow and the iron-shod spud. With the latter he digs roots and spears young wolves and jackals. For the wolves he claims the Government reward; but he often manipulates the head of a jackal to pass muster as that of a wolf. His spud is useful in making an entry through the mud wall of a house, and with it he digs out snakes, field mice, and lizards, all of which he eats. In the Punjab they are said, like the Nats, to divide their women into two classes—the married, who are chaste; the unmarried, who are dissolute.

It is remarkable that these tribes have continued their traditional modes of life and carry on their primitive industries practically unaffected by the culture which for ages has surrounded them. But the example of European Gipsies shows the persistence of nomadic habit, and of the industries which alone are possible in such a course of life. In India, the formation of func-

A Kalwār, or Seller of Spirits (p. 119)

tional groups and the prevailing respect for custom tend to stereotype habits such as these.

It may be asked how far do these primitive industries of the villager and the vagrant yield to modern industrialism? In Bengal, though that country is accessible from the seacoast, they do not seem to have been much disturbed by the new conditions. In the Delta, it is true that the village system has largely given way to individual rights of property, and the coparcenary community, with its roll of servants and menials, has practically disappeared. But in the more backward parts of the province, like Behar and Orissa, the old system of remunerating the village servants still survives. In many places, according to Mr. Gait, the barber, washerman, and blacksmith have each their circle of constituents, and any attempt by one member of a caste to filch away the customers of another is visited with the sharp displeasure of the caste committee. Among Mohammedans these rights are so well established that they devolve by inheritance and often form the dower of a daughter. In Orissa, which is in a more primitive condition even than Behar, it is the custom, when a new village is founded, to attract these menials by grants of rent-free land in addition to the doles of grain and money which they receive.

The state of things in the United Provinces and the Punjab is similar, and Mr. Rose, for the latter province, gives an interesting account of the system. The menials are attached not so much to the village as to the tribe, which has here maintained its influence more successfully than in other parts of the country. So much is this the case that when the tribe migrates, its dependants—Bhāts, Brahmans, or Doms—accompany it. This has recently been the case when the new irrigation colonies were founded on the Chenāb. 'Thus,' Mr. Rose writes, 'each tribe at least, if not each village, was economically a water-tight compartment, self-contained, and independent of the outside world for the necessaries of life; but for commodities not obtainable within its own borders it depended on foreign sources of supply, and on the outside castes, such as Labānas or salt-traders, who formed no part of the tribal or village community. Thus there never have arisen, in this part of India, any great industries. Foreign trade, necessarily confined to the few large towns, was limited to superfluities or luxuries, and such industries as existed were necessarily on a small scale. Further, inasmuch as each community was absolutely independent, as far as necessaries were concerned, the few industries which supplied luxuries never became firmly rooted, and have succumbed at the first breath of competition.'

'Everywhere,' he goes on to say, 'in our official literature one reads of struggling industries in the small towns, though fostered by intermittent official encouragement, dying of inanition. The cause seems obvious enough. Everything essential can be, and for the most part is, made in the village or locality, so that there never is a demand for imported articles of ordinary make, those made by the village artisan, however inferior in quality, satisfying all requirements. In good seasons there is some demand for articles of a better class, but when times are bad that demand ceases and the industry languishes. If the crop is short, every one, from the landlord to the Chūhra, receives a diminished share; but small as the share may be, it is always forthcoming, whereas in the towns the artisan is the first to suffer in times of scarcity, and if the scarcity is prolonged the urban industries are extinguished. But, if on the other hand, these industries are precarious, the village industries are firmly established, and will probably die hard in the face of the increasing competition which menaces them.'

At the same time there is evidence of the decay of the higher village industries, weaving in particular. The manufacture of muslins at Dacca, in Bengal, of shawls in Kashmir, has disappeared, partly owing to repressive duties, and partly to changes in fashion. The large increase of cotton-mills in India itself has acted in the same way. Local-made iron has given way before foreign imports, and many petty articles sold in the village fairs are made in England or in Germany. It is only the very rudest handicrafts which continue to supply the wants of the people.

CHAPTER VIII

HOME LIFE: THE OCCUPATIONS OF WOMEN

The house. A Punjab village described. The cattle. The rest-house. The well and tank. The circles of soil. The year's farming work. The relaxation of the peasant. The work of women—preparation of food. The forest woman and her occupations. The silk industry. The work of the Gipsy woman. The wife of the artisan—spinning, dyeing. Woman as a beast of burden. The care of cattle. Irrigation. Rice-planting. Husking and grinding grain. Cooking.

FROM the village and its industries we pass to the home life of the people.

As a rule, throughout Northern India it is only the landowners, traders, writers, higher artisans, and the more respectable cultivators who live in houses on which any skilled labour has been expended. The walls of such a house are of brick, and outside it is often elaborately decorated with coarse frescoes, which serve as a protection from the Evil Eye.' In the great cities of the west the façade is sometimes ornamented with beautiful carving in stone. But such a house, though grander and costlier than that of the villager, is even less comfortable. The rooms are low and ill-ventilated; the stairs and passages narrow and inconvenient. There is no provision for drainage, and the water-supply is often insanitary. The occupier of such a house keeps his womenkind in seclusion, and the unhealthy conditions under which people of this class pass their lives are apparent in their poor physique, chronic ill-health, and small families.

The walls of the peasant's house are made of mud, or in some places of wattle and dab. The doors are of the rudest kind, and the windows only unglazed apertures in the walls. The roof is sometimes thatched, sometimes tiled, sometimes formed of beams resting on the walls, which support a layer of hardened clay. The outer gate consists of a couple of cross-bars in which thorns are interwoven. The hut of the day-labourer or menial is still ruder—the roof seldom waterproof, the covering of straw, reeds, or sugar-cane leaves resting on light rafters or bamboos. There is no wooden door, the entrance being closed with a screen made of brushwood. The chief risk is that of fire, and when the west winds blow in summer, and everything is as dry as tinder, any carelessness may bring on a conflagration which reduces half a village to ruins. In our eyes these huts, destitute of furniture except a couple of rickety cots, and offering no facilities for the isolation of the sexes, seem miserable in the extreme. But the peasant and his family spend most of their time out of doors, and use breeds familiarity with conditions which would seem intolerable to us, accustomed to the superfluity of so-called comforts which habit compels us to provide.

As an example of village life we may select one of the Punjab villages as described by Messrs. Purser and

Fanshawe. Here each division of the settlement is isolated. Over the main street in which the better houses are situated is hung a string to which is fastened a piece of wood covered with hieroglyphics, a charm provided by some holy Fakīr to keep off cattle disease. The bulk of the population being Mohammedan, the absence of caste restrictions permits a considerable amount of co-operation in the matter of food and cooking. Thus, there will be a common flour-mill worked by one or two oxen, and near it the village Māchi has a fire crackling in the general oven, near which stands a crowd of women with their dishes of dough, waiting till their turn comes to get their cakes baked. Trade and money-lending are in the hands of the Karār, or Hindu merchant, whose house is filled with huge cylinders made of thick ropes of grass, fastened together with pegs and daubed with mud, in which he keeps the grain which he collects at harvest-time in repayment of his loans of seed. He is also interested in cotton, and the beds on which his family sleep at night are used by day for drying the white fibre from which he is extracting the seed with a rude, hand-worked gin.

When we explore an alley and approach the house of a peasant, we find the doorway opening on the street usually handsomely carved. Inside this is a courtyard, where the cattle are shut up at night, and beyond this is the room in which the family live. As we enter, cooking is going on, and there being no chimney, we can only see through the gloom that substantial wooden pillars support the roof. All over the floor brass dishes and pots, spinning-wheels, baskets, and receptacles for grain are scattered about in confusion, while from some hidden recess is heard the subdued murmur of the grinding of a corn-mill. A ladder connects the roof with the ground through a trap-door, and here fodder is stored, cotton and grain are placed to dry, and the family sleep in the hot weather.

The houses of the artisans will be easily recognised from their surroundings—that of the carpenter with wood piled round it; that of the blacksmith with a little furnace close by; the oil-man may have a buffalo at work at his mill; the dyer has skeins of brightly coloured thread hung out to dry, and great earthen pots full of dyes; the pony tied up outside points out the house of the barber; the village trader will be found squatting inside his shop amidst a bewildering collection of grain bags, oil jars, and ledgers, or weighing grain and cleaning cotton in his verandah, or in the space before his shop. On his door-posts he has sundry marks, like that of the red hand, to ward off the Evil Eye. If he be a cloth-seller the gaudy labels from his bales, or a rude picture of a god or of a British soldier serve the same purpose, and scare demons from his property.

These are the respectable craftsmen. Outside the village site is the settlement of the Chamārs, or curriers, with high-smelling tanning vats and skins full of curing stuff hanging from the trees; or that of the weaver with his lines of yarn. The house of the potter may be recognised by piles of clay and potsherds, his kiln, and the ass which he uses as a beast of burden.

Just outside the village site is a plain mud building with three pinnacles on the roof, a platform in front strewed with grass, and surrounded with a mud enclosure. Several water-pots for ablution are placed on the platform, and often there is an oven for heating water. This is the village mosque, used not merely as a house of worship, but as the halting-place for travellers and wandering friars, who are entertained at the expense of the village community. If the proprietors belong to a pious tribe, half a dozen little boys will be seen in the forenoon sitting in front of their teacher, swinging themselves backwards and forwards in a slow rhythm, reciting passages of the Korān at the top of their voices, while the master follows the recitation with the holy volume placed on a stand before him. The artisans of the village are all at work in the open air—a few weavers making cloth, a carpenter mending the cogs of a Persian wheel, the blacksmith forging the coulter of a plough.

The village abounds in animal life. Every house has one or more yokes of oxen, cows, and, buffaloes, the last found chiefly in villages occupied by tribes like the Ahīrs and Gūjars, who make their living by manufacturing ghi. Goats of the fine, dignified local breed are to be found everywhere; but sheep are kept only by the Gadaria caste, who graze them on the rough pasture which is to be procured only in the wilder tracts. Pigs, animals foul in the eyes of both Hindus and Mohammedans, are found only in the hovels of the menial castes. Cowardly yelping curs abound, with a sort of trades-union of their own, each quarter of the village being occupied by a separate pack. The wealthier residents have dogs of their own, which they supply with food; but the majority are ownerless, feeding on the garbage flung upon the refuse-heaps, and disputing with the vultures and jackals for the bodies of dead cattle which are cast away on the outskirts of the settlement.

The social life of the village centres round the travellers' rest-house, which is found most fully developed in the Punjab and in the United Provinces. In the former province it is a building of some pretensions. In the latter it consists merely of a shed or line of sheds, outside which is a platform supplied with cots, wooden benches, cooking-pots, and tobacco-pipes for the use of strangers, each of the last being marked by a coloured rag to denote that it is reserved for a certain group of castes. Visitors to the village are entertained here at the public expense, and it is the halting-place of the wandering Fakīr and other ne'er-do-weels of his kind. Here the police-officer conducts his investigations when a crime is committed; the landlord collects his rents; the village council sits to deal with breaches of morality or violation of caste rules. When a girl in the village is married the procession of the bridegroom is accommodated here, and in the evening the worthies assemble to smoke, gossip, and discuss local politics.

The well and the tank occupy the same place in the women's life. Early in the morning you may watch lines of them passing to and fro from their houses with the full or empty clay or brass water-pots poised on their heads in a fashion which among no race of women is more graceful than with those of India. The little children cling to their mothers' skirts as they go for water, and dabble their tiny feet in the water as the matrons fill their jars. The water of the tank, which is used for both ablution and drinking, is a much less healthful source of supply than the well. This in the spring is a scene of active life, the great oxen hauling up the water-bags, while the stream is diverted through many channels into the fields, where the women and children distribute it into the tiny plots.

Beyond the village site, practically the whole area is devoted to the plough. Looking down on the cultivated tract from the mound on which the village houses are planted, it is generally possible to distinguish at least three concentric rings, or circles of soil, each of which has a different economic value. Close to the settlement is the tract which has been longest under cultivation, carefully irrigated and heavily manured. Here are grown the more valuable crops—sugar-cane and poppy, cotton, vegetables, and the like. Beyond this is the middle circle, less fertile, less fully irrigated and manured. This is sown with cereals, rice or wheat, barley, millets, and pulses in infinite variety. Lastly, on the outskirts of the village area is the least valuable ring. Little manure and irrigation are applied to this, and on account of its distance from the village site, it is exposed to theft, trespass, and damage by wild pigs, deer, monkeys, and birds. Hence nearly every field has its platform on which the owner keeps watch while the crops are ripening. During the day he is relieved by his wife and children, who fling clods of earth from slings and pellet-bows, and keep up a constant shouting and clattering of rattles to scare the green parrots and other birds. The cattle are grazed during the day in the small piece of commonage, under the care of a gang of boys and girls. But the grass supply is insufficient to keep them in working condition, and they must be fed at the stall with stalks of millet cut into lengths with a chopper, or with the chaff collected after the oxen have trodden out the grain. When the crop is ripe it is cut, bound into loads, and carried at once to the common threshing-floor, where each tenant's crop is piled in a separate heap. When dry it is spread out and trodden by a team of oxen moving slowly round a centre post. All this time the owner must watch it carefully day and night, to protect it from theft and fire raised either by accident or by the malice of an enemy, who thus takes his revenge for some insult or injury. The grain is winnowed by throwing it into the air with shovels, or by letting it fall from baskets when the strong west wind which ushers in the hot season begins to blow. The cleaned grain is then collected, the doles payable to the village servants are deducted from it, and the balance is stored in granaries within the hut, or sold at once if the market be favourable, or the landlord press for his rent. The chaff for the feed of the working cattle is piled in a heap, which is thatched to save it from rain.

The work of the year varies with the climate and the different modes of husbandry. In the Bengal delta, a land of rice, there are two main crops—the broadcast and inferior variety being sown with the first fall of rain; the transplanted and superior kind, for which a nursery is prepared and the seedlings removed from it to the fields. Further west the husbandry is more varied. Here there are two harvests—that of millets, maize, and cotton sown and gathered in the autumnal rainy season; that of wheat, barley, peas, and various pulses and oil-seeds sown at the close of the monsoon, and reaped in the spring. Sugar-cane, a most important and valuable crop, is sown in the spring, and cut and crushed after standing in the field for nearly a year.

The area of land which can be worked by a single family and one pair of oxen varies greatly. To the east of the United Provinces and in Behar, for instance, such a farm would contain four or five acres; but the average is greater where rice, which needs less ploughing than other cereals, is in excess. Where the habit of growing two crops within the year prevails, the work of the farmer begins about July, when the autumn crops, millets, maize, or cotton, are sown. These need continuous weeding, and whenever the weather is open the ploughing for the spring crop goes on. Meanwhile, as the rain crops ripen, they must be carefully watched to save them from birds and other enemies, and they are finally harvested after October, when the monsoon clears. Then the spring sowings begin, and as they grow, irrigation from well, tank, or canal must go on,

No. 18

Weavers at Work (p. 136)

particularly if the welcome fall of rain about Christmas time should fail. By the beginning of March the wheat and barley are ripe, and the harvesting, threshing, and storing of the grain occupy the next month or two. Thus the toil and anxieties of the farmer are continuous, and his only period of comparative rest is in the heavy rain time, when, as he says, the god Vishnu goes to sleep, and does not wake till October is well advanced and the time has come to begin cutting and crushing the sugar-cane and boiling down the juice.

You may watch him in the working season as he starts at sunrise, with his plough over his shoulder, and driving his pair of lean oxen before him. If work be pressing, he and his hired men pass the day in the fields, eating at noon the simple meal which one of his little girls brings to him from the house. After a siesta in the shade and a pipe he resumes his work, and returns in the evening, the 'time of the cows' dust,' as he calls it, when the cattle come home from pasture, and the air is thick with the dust which they raise in the narrow field-paths. If work be light, he dines at home, bathes at the village well, and enjoys the luxury of doing nothing, which no one in the world loves so well. Then the day closes with a smoke and a chat at the village rest-house. Stretched on a mat or crazy cot, he sleeps the sleep of fatigue, heedless of the howls of the jackals on the outskirts of the village answered by the pack of pariah curs which support themselves on rubbish and carrion. The care of his fields is ever on his mind. The amount of rain and the periods at which it falls may suit one crop and ruin another. Hence the man who adopts the plan of mixed husbandry is more likely to escape utter ruin than he who depends upon a single staple.

It is a dull, monotonous life. He has little knowledge of the great world save that which he picks up when he goes on a pilgrimage, or is summoned to attend the courts as a party or witness in a case. The village and its petty concerns supply his only subject of conversation, except when a wandering friar halts at the village rest-house, and describes to a wondering audience the marvels which he has seen. Literature is unknown to him, save when he listens to a folk-tale told round the fire kindled in the open on a winter evening, or hears the occasional recital of a religious book or ballad. But hard as his lot often is, he is quite content if he can escape the greater evils, famine and pestilence; if he has means to marry his children and perform the death rites for his relations according to the usages of his caste. At other times he is satisfied to stroll round his fields and watch the springing or the ripening crops and the great white oxen chewing the cud at the stall.

There is no more variety in the life of the woman than in that of the man. Marriage, which is the destiny of every member of the sex, except those who are hopelessly crippled or unhealthy, is the great event of her life. To arrange the marriage of his daughters is the most pressing duty of a father. No scandal is so grievous as that which results from the presence of a grown-up, unmarried daughter in the house. But marriage, as will be seen, involves greater difficulty than in western lands, because the restrictions which surround the selection of a partner are so numerous and intricate that the field of choice is very narrowly defined, and if a child is to be suitably mated, the engagement must be made in childhood, and neither party is permitted to indulge his or her inclinations.

The occupations of women furnish a subject of much interest and importance. Women's work generally may be divided into three classes—first, independent labour; secondly, that which is supplementary to the husband's work; lastly, that which is common to both sexes. But the conditions of life and the statistical returns of occupations do not enable us to distinguish these classes. At a census it has generally been found possible only to record the sole or more important occupation of the head of the family, and to class the other members of the household as dependent upon him. In other words, the specialisation of labour which is inevitable under the caste organisation and the close family system tend to check the independence of the subordinate members. The wife may practise some minor industry, such as spinning, by which she supplements the family income, but she will almost inevitably be recorded as assisting in her husband's occupation.

It will be convenient to discuss women's labour in connection with the wide divisions of industry—those of the agriculturist, the jungle-dweller, the artisan.

One class of work, however, and that the most

important, is among all classes entrusted to women—the provision and preparation of food. In the case of the forest and Gipsy tribes, as with all savages and semi-savages, the collection of food and cooking are essentially women's duties. The pursuit of game, on the other hand, is the business of the men. Among the Santāls, however, the woman plays her part in hunting, but it is confined to promoting, by a sort of sympathetic magic, the success of her husband. Mr. Bradley-Birt tells us that when a man goes on the chase he binds his wife lightly hand and foot, and lays her on a cot, with her face pointing towards the centre of the hut. She must remain in this position, staring into a bowl of water, until, through some hypnotic concentration of thought, she sees its contents turn into blood. Once this miracle is performed, she may go about her work, knowing that all is well with the hunters.

In the central hill tracts the woman collects with her digging-spud many kinds of wild vegetable food. Some tubers which are poisonous or unwholesome she renders nutritious by washing or soaking in water. Among the fruits or berries which she procures by far the most important is the Mohwa (*Bassia latifolia*), a fine tree which gives the country something of the appearance of an English park. The fruit, as well as the fleshy corolla, is edible, and furnishes the main food of the poorer classes for several months. As spring comes on and the flowers are fully developed, the corollas become turgid, gradually drop from the calix, and fall to the ground in a snowy shower.

Before the crop has begun to fall the grass and leaves at the foot of the tree are burnt to facilitate collection. Then the women and children start for the place at dawn, and remain there all day, sometimes sleeping and sometimes collecting the flowers. The men visit the grove once or twice in the day and carry off what has been collected. At night the animals and birds claim their share, and cattle are so fond of it that at the Mohwa season the milk acquires a special flavour. It has been estimated by Dr. Ball that 160 lbs. of Mohwa flowers will supply a month's food to a family of five persons. It is seldom eaten alone, but is mixed with the seeds of the Sāl (*Shorea robusta*), or with the leaves of certain jungle plants, to which a small quantity of rice is sometimes added. It is the custom to cook it only once a day, and each member of the family helps himself to it when he feels hungry.

This is the most primitive kind of food-supply procurable by these jungle-folk. But when it is abundant it leads to the beginnings of commercialism; Mohwa being largely used in the plains for the distillation of the crudest variety of native spirits, traders enter the forest country and obtain it from the tribes by purchase or barter.

During times of scarcity in the plains women may be seen collecting in a sort of sieve-basket the seeds of a species of wild rice or other grasses, which, though possessing little nutriment, can still be used to eke out their scanty rations. They also gather for pottage the leaves of various leguminous plants, which in certain seasons form an important part of the family food. When the bamboo flowers, as it often does in dry seasons, the seeds are used in the same way.

When we pass from the provision of food to the beginnings of industrialism, the Tusser silk industry at one of its stages gives scope to the labour of women. The forest tribes of the central hills collect the cocoons in the early months of the rainy season. These are sold to professional rearers, who attach them to selected trees of the Sāj (*Terminalia tormentosa*). By and by the moths cut through the cocoons, and after they have paired, the females are placed in earthen pots in which they lay their eggs and die. The eggs are incubated by heat, and the worms after a time form new cocoons which are sold to merchants from the plains. In this process of semi-domestication the men are required to observe the rule of purity, to confine their diet to rice and salt, to fee the Baiga priest to pray for the welfare of the crop, and to permit no woman to approach the hut in which the breeding is carried on. It is in the subsequent process of reeling and dyeing the silk that women are employed. This distribution of work between the sexes is a curious example of the effect of taboo upon industry.

This taboo of women does not extend to other forest products. They are engaged in the collection of the resinous incrustation formed on the twigs of certain trees by the Lac insect, which is found in more or less abundance in the central hills. Thence it is exported to places like Mirzapur, where it is melted and purified in an ingenious way, and becomes the shellac of commerce.

This is only one of the many products of the same kind collected by women. The Myrobolans of commerce, known also as gall-nuts, are gathered for use in both tanning and dyeing, and every native bazaar supports an Attār, or native druggist, who is generally in collusion with the Hakīm, or physician, and lives by preparing the nauseous concoctions containing various wild flowers, herbs, leaves, fruits, nuts, and roots, which he purchases from the jungle women who collect them.

Passing from the forest tribes to the Gipsy-like races of the plains, we come on another set of industries in which women are largely employed. The Nat women, as we have seen, make a speciality of tattooing. Next come the Dom and his kinsfolk, who work in bamboo, out of which they make fans, mats, and basketry. Dom women make the coarse bamboo matting which in European houses protects the carpets from the ravages of the white ants. This is made *in situ*, a party of women bringing their slips of cane and weaving the mat to suit the size and shape of the room. All kinds of basketry are made by these women, from the large crates in which the women of the grain-parcher's household collect the dry leaves with which he fires his oven, or the cumbrous baskets used on the threshing-floor, down to those of small size for household use. Some of these small baskets, made of slips of rattan cane, are artistic and pretty, but they never reach the skill displayed by the American Indian women, as described in Mr. Mason's admirable monograph. Some, again, work in the stalks of reeds, out of which they make tilts for wagons, the curious Morha, or hour-glass-shaped stool, the pattern of which comes down from the ancient Hindu throne, or the neat little winnowing-fan with which women clean the grain. Rope-making from various kinds of fibre is also an industry of women, in so far that they scutch the fibre which the men twist into rope.

In manufactures of a higher class women work more in the collection and preparation of the material than in the final stages. The potter's wife digs the clay for her husband, and paints the pots with streaks of colour before they are baked. The women of the glass-bangle maker's household pack his fragile wares. In the industries connected with wool and cotton, the picking and scutching of the fibre are entrusted to women. Spinning is one of the few crafts which are independent of caste restrictions, and in a well-regulated peasant family there should be a wheel for every female in the family, and little girls are carefully instructed in the art by their mothers (Pl. 30). The wheel itself, which closely resembles that of Europe, is a clumsy, but effective machine. The mother-in-law has much difficulty in keeping the young married women steadily at work on this monotonous task, and most of the real spinning work is done by some old crone, or by a widow who is the general family drudge.

The palmy days of cotton-spinning are over. In his classical account of the manufacture of Dacca muslins, Mr. Taylor describes how the fine thread was made in the early part of the last century. The cotton was

Carpenters at Work (p. 134)

first hand-picked, and then the women, 'with the unwearied patience which characterises the race,' proceeded to remove the fine wool from each individual seed with the jaw-bone of the Boalli, a Ganges fish. Next the fibre was placed on a board and rolled gently backwards and forwards with an iron pin, and teased with a small elastic bow. The downy fleece thus produced was shaped by being lapped round a wooden roller, pressed between two boards, rolled on a piece of lacquered reed the size of a quill, and finally enveloped in a piece of soft fish-skin to prevent it from being soiled while held in the hand during the process of spinning.

Of the Hindu women spinners, one of Mr. Taylor's authorities says that 'they have a delicacy of touch which apparently compensates for their want of strength, beyond any nation on the face of the earth'; another states that their 'temperament possesses every feature of that termed nervous by physiologists.' The finest thread was spun by women under thirty years of age. The apparatus was kept in a flat work-basket, and comprised the cylindrical roll of cotton, a delicate spindle, sometimes made of iron, sometimes of a slender piece of bamboo, a piece of shell embedded in clay, and a little hollow stone containing chalk powder, in which the spinner occasionally dipped her fingers. The spindle was about the thickness of a stout needle, and near its point was attached a ball of unbaked clay to give it the weight necessary to cause it to revolve. Similar spindle-whorls of a larger size have been found on the oldest inhabited sites in the country. The work could be done only in a moist atmosphere, like that of Dacca. The finest yarn was made in the early morning, before the sun dried the dew. At other times the spinning was done over a shallow dish of water, the evaporation from which produced the necessary moisture. It required a microscope to detect any inequality in the thread.

As regards dyeing, women are specially skilled in the ingenious method by which the spotted cloth, known in Northern India as Chūnri, is made. The cloth to be dyed is washed and folded. The places where the spots are intended to be are tied up with threads in the form of screws—a process requiring ingenuity and practical skill. The cloth is then dipped in the dye. When taken out it is dried, with the result that the knotted parts remain white, while the rest of the material is coloured.

The Indian woman is the chief carrier and beast of burden. She draws water from the well; carries the sheaves to the threshing-floor; bears loads of wood, chaff, fuel, or vegetables, for sale in cities.

One of her main duties is the tending of cattle. When still a little girl she drives the cows to pasture, is trained to milk them, and prepare Dahi, or curds, and Ghi, or clarified butter.

She also does much field-work, such as lifting the water with a scoop from one reservoir to another until at last it reaches the level from which it is distributed to the fields. In the rice districts it is the men who plough and plant the nurseries, while the women transplant the seedlings in the sloppy mud. Mr. Gore gives a lively account of this work in the Kulu valley. 'Musicians are got together, and soon the rows of laughing girls with kilted skirts are standing up to their knees in mud and water planting the bright green shoots in the soft ground at their feet. It must be hard work, this stooping all day in the hot sun, but the work goes on merrily to the weird sound of the music and the drum. The singers chant of love, always in the minor key, to the running commentary of the light-hearted girls, who emphasise each point with many a joke upon their comely neighbours, while the bystanders lose no opportunity of throwing in a rough jest to raise the colour in the cheeks of the girls before them.' In this district and elsewhere woman is looked on simply as a labour-saving machine. The same writer met a man who was generally regarded as a smart fellow. He bought a wife cheap, broke her in to be a useful worker at home and in the field, and then sold her for double the money she originally cost. This, indeed, seemed to be his business, for he was then in process of educating the third.

Woman's most laborious work is that of husking and grinding grain. The rice is cleaned in a wooden mortar, in which it is pounded with a heavy wooden pestle. It is healthy work, and produces a fine physical development in those accustomed to the exercise. Grinding flour is much more laborious, because the rice-husker stands as she works, while the woman at the mill has to adopt a stooping, strained position. Women start flour-grinding in the last watch of the night, and riding through a village in the grey dawn you will hear the creaking of the querns, and the low, sad song of the women. In the Punjab hills water-power is utilised for this purpose, and the mills in the Kurram valley are sacred to the women. 'It is they,' says Mr. Gore, 'who carry the corn thither in baskets, grind it, and carry it home again. The mill thus becomes the centre round which the love-stories play. Assignations are made here, and if the ardent lover is bold enough, he carries off the loved one as she returns in the dusk with her load gracefully poised on her head.'

Everywhere much of the housewife's time is taken up in boiling the rice and pulse, or making the wheat and barley bannocks which are the usual food of the peasantry. In a small cultivator's family no attempt is made to provide variety in the menu. The people are as conservative in food as in clothing. The monuments show that the materials and fashion of dress are much the same as they were two thousand years ago. The case is the same with the diet of the Hindu, and it is only in the use of varied spices and condiments, or in sweetmeats which are always purchased, that there is any variety. In the case of the richer classes the only difference is that the food is rendered indigestible by a lavish use of butter and vegetable oil. Hence the rich banker and his womenkind suffer from chronic dyspepsia. The Hindu woman often cooks excellent vegetable curries; but the curry and pulao of the Mohammedan is much more tasty and nutritious because she has a larger range of materials, in particular of meat.

In the Punjab, says Mr. Rose, 'women, when

employed at all, or allowed to earn a living, must work at the most degrading and roughest occupations.' Such is the manufacture of fuel, converting the cow manure into cakes with an admixture of chaff and other refuse, and plastering them on a sunny wall to dry.

The work in the opium field is perhaps the most pleasant of women's tasks. She escapes the stuffiness of her hut and works in the open air at the finest season of the year. As the petals fall off she collects them, and presses them with a damp cloth until the resinous matter which they contain makes them adhere firmly together. When the ball of opium is made for export it is pressed into a brass cup lined with these petal cakes, which are afterwards stiffened by painting them with the juice of the drug. This gives to the opium that hay-like smell which the Chinese connoisseur appreciates. It is said that this is one of the few cases in which the sex in India is allowed to appropriate a little perquisite for pocket-money. When the capsules are ripe they are pierced and the opium is collected with a little iron scoop, a small mussel shell, or a piece of bamboo. This work of collection is done principally by women and children.

Thus the peasant woman, from early dawn to nightfall, is kept busily employed in preparing food, looking after her babies, tending the cattle, spinning, and doing such field-work as she is able to perform. Her only relaxations are the chat with her cronies at the well or tank, and the pipe which she loves as much as her husband. She is a cheery, hard-working creature, devoted to the care of her household as she understands it. If her moral sense is vague, her language coarse, her person less clean than might be desired—these faults are largely due to her environment, and those who know her best learn to respect her many virtues.

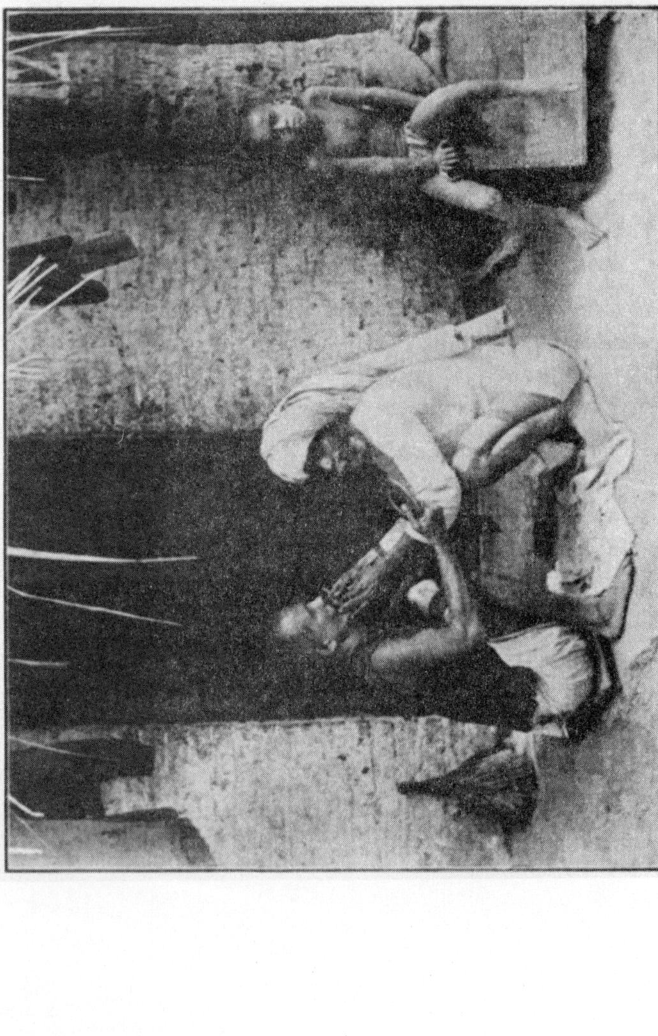

A Barber Shaving a Mourner (p. 217)

CHAPTER IX

CHILD LIFE: GAMES AND AMUSEMENTS

Mystery of Indian child life. Isolation of children from Europeans. Lack of reverence. Sedateness, ease of manner. Etiquette. Conventions regarding children. Marriage arrangements. Pampering of children. Occupation of peasant children. Knowledge of Nature. Imaginativeness. Training of girls. Infant marriage, its origin and results. The mother-in-law. Training of boys. Amusements. Dancing. Persistence of habit. Tip-cat. Prisoners' Base. Leap-frog. Blind-man's Buff. Feats of strength and skill. Gulli Danda. Girls' games. Dolls. Mimic marriages. Floating away ill-luck.

THE world of Indian child life is generally a mystery to the European, even to those who have spent a large portion of their life in the country. Between him and the native woman a great gulf is fixed, and she enforces the same restrictions on his intercourse with her children. This is partly due to the fact that she is more conservative in her modes of thought than her men folk, and is less disposed than they are to enter into friendly relations with a stranger. Again, on account of her isolation from the European, she has come to regard him as specially uncanny, a person whose novel dress and language, manners, and customs, and in particular his contempt for the conventions of eating and drinking which form one of the chief interests of her life, suggest that he may cast the Evil Eye upon her children, or injure them in other ways. How far this feeling of aloofness may give way to increased education and culture is doubtful. The problem of improving the social relations of the white and dark races is one of immense practical difficulty, the solution of which will require much tactful management, but the concessions necessary to bring about harmony must not be confined to Europeans. At present it is only a lady like Miss Sorabji, born in the land and familiar with the customs and prejudices of the people, who can gain first-hand knowledge of babies and their ways.

What strikes one first, looking at them over the barrier which custom erects between the foreigner and native children, is their precocity. There is no nursery in the Indian home, and from the time when the children begin to toddle about they share in the family life. In households of the upper class where the ladies are secluded, even the little girls have the run of the men's quarters, where the owner receives his friends, until they reach the age when their marriage is being arranged, and they are compelled to retire behind the purdah. In the household of the peasant the family lives chiefly in the open air, and the children of both sexes play together in the village lanes. Hence little mites come to know much more of the evil world and of its ways than children of the same age in western lands. To quote Miss Billington: 'Innocent in the sense understood of European children they never are, for reticence and mystery towards them are quite unknown, and one might almost say that they babble artlessly over subjects that elderly matrons at home would discuss under all reservation. The knowledge of, and admission of, this fact is absolutely necessary for the comprehension of much that seems puzzling and suggestive of moral degradation in the Indian character. A knowledge of what one may euphemistically write of as "the facts of life" gives the women a habit of thought which makes them seem perfectly natural and everyday things, and as such they discuss them, but not merely from a morbid love of nauseous detail as those who do not understand at once define it to be.' This lack of reticence is one of the predominant notes of peasant life. The hut provides no facilities for privacy or for the isolation of the sexes, and the fact of belonging to a close corporation, like a caste or tribe, presupposes that the brethren are ignorant of little that goes on in each other's households. Gossip and the petty squabbles of husband and wife, or of two rival wives, are conducted *coram populo* in the open air, and become the common property of the neighbourhood. Such incidents give occasion for shameless indecency of abuse which the children learn from the age when they begin to understand anything.

With this precocity is combined a more imaginative view of life than that which our children ever reach. The atmosphere is full of the supernatural—evil-minded ghosts and bogies, the kindly spirits of the ancestral dead which sit round the hearth, the ogre and vampire which haunt the burial-ground or the old village trees

—with all of which the child, even in infancy, becomes acquainted. The tales which our matter-of-fact babies only half believe are realities to him, and he sees no incongruity in recognising the magician who can turn a man into an ox, or a tiger which is able to speak.

The practical rules of life, again, are enforced even in early childhood. Little children learn the importance of obeying the laws of their caste, the taboo on food cooked otherwise than by the prescribed methods, the rules which define what is lucky and unlucky, and, most important of all, the myriad conventions connected with Dastūr, the customary rites and habits which have descended from remote antiquity, and are treasured and observed by each succeeding generation. On this regard for prescription is largely based the profound conservatism of the people, their dislike of novelty and change, the monotonous round of daily life, the observance of primitive fashions in food, dress, and ornament.

All this early training tends to promote that sedateness, ease of manner, and what we should call 'old-fashioned' ways of thought and action which are so characteristic of Indian children. They seem to be grown up while they are mere babies, and they have little of the gaucherie and shyness of our youths or of girls before they have begun to 'put up their hair.' In a land where the observance of elaborate etiquette is a serious object of life, the little boy in a respectable family is trained at an early age to observe its rules. The native gentleman, for instance, carefully follows the prescribed routine of 'sitting and rising,' as he terms it. There is a right and a wrong way of sitting on a chair in the presence of a guest or of a superior. A well-bred man must not loll, but sit straight; he must not fling his legs about carelessly, but draw them in beneath him; he must not leave his knees exposed, but arrange the skirts of his upper garment decorously above them. So with the salaam, which is carefully regulated to express the degree of respect due to stranger or visitor. In receiving a guest it is a question of the highest importance whether his rank requires that he should or should not be met at the door, assisted to alight from his carriage, and conducted respectfully to his seat. During the visit the mutual congratulations and inquiries about health follow a well-defined course, any divergence from which may be taken as an insult, or be sneered at as a sign of boorishness and low birth. It is only the educated young man who, with the pseudo-independence of an English board-school boy, neglects conventions such as these. But in a well-regulated Indian family they are carefully explained to the boy as soon as he passes the stage of infancy, and he, with the imitative faculty of his race, soon learns to copy the manners of his father and his guests. Thus the well-bred child soon acquires a dignity of bearing and ease of manner which are admirable in their way.

The zenana, too, no less than the men's apartments, has its conventions and rules of etiquette, and when the lady friends of the mistress of the house pay formal calls, the emissaries arrive to settle a match, or the wives of the brethren attend to offer their condolences on the occasion of a death or other misfortune, the little girls are carefully trained to take their part in the ceremonial in a fitting way.

In connection with this regard for etiquette as it affects the upper classes, it must be remembered that one of the most stringent conventions is that it is dangerous for a visitor to inquire about the health of the children, still more dangerous to praise their beauty, dress, or ornaments. Praise of this kind is believed to bring a Nemesis with it, or it may suggest the envious glance of the malignant. If you do praise a child, some precaution, such as cracking the finger joints, should be taken, or among Mohammedans the remark is accompanied by some pious ejaculation, which acts as a protective. The ladies of the household, and particularly unmarried girls who have reached the time of life at which they are secluded, can only be referred to cautiously, and that by intimate friends. In any case they are spoken of by some euphemistic title—'the veiled ones,' 'the house folk,' and so on.

Conventions and etiquette such as these have little place in the peasant's life. It is only when a marriage or other family rite is being performed that they regulate his actions. And here it may be noted that caste is in some ways a very democratic institution. Rank and wealth, of course, have their influence in India as elsewhere; but the poor village Brahman looks down on the wealthy banker or pawnbroker, expects a salute from him when they meet, and when he visits the house of the rich man, he shows by every word and act that his arrival is a piece of condescension, and that he is fully aware that he risks personal pollution by entering the dwelling of a man whose caste is lower than his own. In arranging a marriage the same feeling prevails. Alliances are made not on the ground of social position and wealth, but because the parties fulfil the conditions of descent which make a union between them possible. A rich landholder naturally seeks a wealthy bride for his son; but from the scarcity of brides and complications in regard to the prohibited degrees, he may have to marry him in a family of low position, and provide the marriage expenses himself. When the marriage day comes he finds the friends of the bride just as conscious of their own dignity arising from descent, and just as sensitive and punctilious as he would be himself.

The children in families of rank give one the impression of being ridiculously coddled and pampered. Nothing is so valuable to a Hindu as a male heir, and without a boy in the house he regards life as a failure. The wife who has failed to perform her most necessary duty, and has remained childless, is an object of contempt, while both she and her husband have serious grounds for looking on their prospects in the next world with anxiety. Hence when the boy arrives he becomes the household pet, and it is impossible to take too much care of him, or do too much to promote his ease and comfort. Such a mode of bringing up a child would necessarily, we should suppose, produce dangerous results in making him headstrong, wilful, and disobedient to his parents. As a matter of fact, this does not happen, partly through the kindly nature of the people themselves, and partly, because reverence to parents is one of the leading principles of that popular morality enforced not so much by religion as by custom. Until the boys go out into the world and set up households of their own, there are few Hindu families in which the younger generation fail to treat the house master with respect. Girls, of course, are less desired than boys, and though they may not be so carefully tended, they seem to suffer little actual ill-treatment. In fact, you will see the peasant father with his little girl babies in his arms and obviously proud of them.

As the son of the landowner and merchant is at the very earliest age introduced to life, and allowed to share in the pursuits and amusements of his seniors, so the child of the peasant, as soon as the stage of making mud pies has passed, is initiated into the craft or occupation of his father. The son of the carpenter, blacksmith, or weaver is soon taught to assist at the bench or forge or in laying out the warp. Among the farming classes the children after babyhood has passed are occupied in various ways. The little boys and girls take the cows and goats to pasture, and are held responsible that they do not trespass in the neighbouring fields, few of which are ever fenced. As they start in the morning they are given a drink of sour milk or whey and a stale cake or two for their midday dinner. This they always supplement with coarse fruit or berries in their season, such as the wild plum, the

No. 21

SNAKE-CHARMERS (p. 187)

corollas of the Mohwa, or other less nutritious products of the jungle. During the main operations of the farm, they are employed in the lighter tasks of distributing water in the seed-beds, weeding or bird-scaring, gleaning and carrying the bundles to the threshing-floor.

This outdoor life forms the child's introduction to that knowledge of Nature and her ways which he is constantly extending in later years. As he drives the cattle to pasture in the grey dawn he watches the wolf or jackal returning from his nightly expeditions, the vultures hovering overhead on the look-out for carrion, the wild-fowl wheeling in flight from one tank to another, the monkeys planning a raid on the standing crops, the squirrels darting along the branches of the trees. Every hedge and copse is full of animal or bird life. The child knows where the wild boar has his lair in the reeds, the hole of the snake under the old banyan-tree. The habits of all the wild fauna he soon learns to understand. He looks at them with a placid enjoyment of their freedom and beauty, and, if he be a true Hindu, he spares and protects them. Unlike the English boy, he never dreams of destroying the pretty creatures or of bird-nesting. This is left to the hunting or Gipsy tribes. But even they seldom destroy animals for the mere pleasure of taking life, but regard them solely as a source of food. Sometimes they will catch birds and bring them into a city, where tender-hearted women, or merchants of the Jain sect, as an act of charity, give him a present on condition that he releases them.

The peasant boy's knowledge of the plant-world is equally wide. In particular, the forest tribes know every berry and root, and the herbs and simples which are useful in medicine. There are hundreds of varieties of rice and other cereals which the ryot can identify with certainty, and his vocabulary, though limited in the characterisation of things which do not come under his daily observation, or do not form subjects which are frequently discussed, blossoms out into a wealth of terms to express all the kinds of grain or plants, the processes of agriculture, the implements and their parts which are in common use.

It is to these quiet days of early boyhood spent under the shade that the peasant owes much of his curious imaginativeness. This is supplemented by the folk-lore learnt round the winter fire, and serves as half his religion. Thus, too, he acquires that love for aphorisms in which he rivals the Spanish peasant. The operations of his field, the laws of weather, the points of cattle, the varieties of produce, jibes at the manners and customs of other castes, and the few simple maxims which govern his conduct he turns into pithy rhymed couplets which display more wit and turn for epigram than we find in the scanty literature which reaches him. This consists of a few chapbooks, the current folk-tales, and an occasional recitation of the fine epic of the Ramayana, translated into his vernacular speech by the genius of Tulsi Das, which more than any other of his religious books may be described as the Bible of Northern India.

In the same way the little girl is trained in household work. She is taught the peculiar knack, not easy to acquire, by which, with a dexterous turn of her wrist, she can sift the grain free of seeds and dirt in the winnowing-fan. She learns the art of milking a cow, and the making of butter and curds, which last forms such a large part of the daily diet; how to boil rice and pulse, how to make a barley or wheaten bannock; how to use the spinning-wheel. It is not her mother, but her grandmother, or some widow in the house, who looks after her training in these matters, because it needs a sharp tongue and steady discipline to teach her the little housewifery she acquires before her married life begins.

Infant marriage is found to prevail only slightly in the Punjab, but increases rapidly as we move south and west, until it reaches its maximum in Behar or Western Bengal. Much has been said against the custom, and it undoubtedly abridges the short, happy period of childhood before the girl has to undertake the responsibilities of housekeeping and motherhood. She has hardly ceased to sport in the village lane and attend to her dolls before her parents arrange her marriage, the main object of her life. Obviously there is little time left for education, and the school inspectress laments that the little maids leave her charge before their training has barely started. Hence she is taught to despise book-learning, and there is no room in Hindu society for the unattached woman, who deliberately abandons the hope of marriage and of rearing a family. There is no career open to her as a clerk, artist, typist, or secretary. Even domestic service is barred to her, and the Ayah of the English lady is always drawn from the scavenger class, or is a Mohammedan. It is true that factories and mines employ much female labour, but this is undertaken by widows or by young women without families, and in the case of the married woman such occupations are regarded as subsidiary to her true mission, and are abandoned when they interfere with household duties and the care of a family.

The evils of the custom of infant marriage have probably been exaggerated. When people speak of physical degeneration it is sufficient to point to races like the Sikhs and Rajputs, among whom it prevails, and who certainly show no signs of decadence. Here the so-called infant marriage is really a betrothal, and married life does not begin until the girl has come of age. It prevails as widely, perhaps more widely, among the lower than among the higher castes in the plains; but it may be assumed that the former have borrowed it from the latter. It does not prevail among the forest tribes, where the bride is very often older than her husband, and it is clearly not one of the primitive institutions of the Indian races, but rather forced upon them by Brahman influence.

Brahmans account for it on the ground that marriage is a sacrament, 'of which,' to use Mr. Risley's words, 'every maiden must partake in order that she may cleanse her own being from the taint of original sin, that she may accomplish the salvation of her father and his ancestors, and that she may bring forth a son to carry on the domestic worship in her husband's family.' This explains why she should be married; not why she should be married as a child. The Brahman theory that the sooner she undertakes these mystic functions the better, is clearly an *ex post facto* explanation. Nor does it help us to explain it as resulting from communal marriage and the capture of wives—the girl being made over to her husband lest she may be appropriated by her kinsmen, or carried off as a slave. There is no evidence of communal marriage in Northern India, and the influence of marriage by capture has been greatly exaggerated.

Mr. Risley with more reason suggests that 'where family interests were involved it may well have seemed simpler to get a girl married before she had developed a will of her own, than to court domestic difficulties by allowing her to grow up and fall in love on her own account. The gradual lowering of the position of women from the ideal standard of Vedic times, and the distrust of their virtue induced by the example of the pre-matrimonial licence set by the Dravidian races must also have had its effect, and, as is not obscurely hinted in the literature of the subject, a girl would be married as a child in order to avoid the possibility of her causing scandal later on.' To this was added the custom of hypergamy, which limits the number of possible husbands for the girls of the higher classes, and thus compels the parents to secure appropriate bridegrooms as soon as possible.

Much has been made of the occasional horrid cases of cruelty to girl brides, which appear in the law reports. Brutality of this kind is found chiefly in

Bengal. But as far as North-western India is concerned, one has only to watch the crowds of laughing girls on their way to a bathing fair, or dipping in the sacred water of the Ganges, or to observe them day by day in an up-country village, to satisfy one's self that their lot cannot be very hard after all.

The bogie of the young bride is, of course, her mother-in-law. The girl comes under her charge before her character is formed, and before she knows much of the mysteries of housewifery. Her chaperon strongly disapproves of any tendency towards flirtation, of education, and of modern ideas of any kind which suggest the licence of the Hetaira. So the girl is carefully watched, and anything in the shape of frivolity is sternly prohibited. She is not at all the innocent young creature she pretends to be, and the old dame is obliged to keep a watchful eye upon her, and see that she is busy at cookery or spinning, not so much because her labour is valuable, but rather to prevent the possibility of scandal. No doubt a girl of lively disposition does sometimes have a hard time, and she is not released from her bondage until she has provided an heir to her husband. After that she is emancipated, she becomes mistress of the house, the mother-in-law is deposed, and the young wife can do much as she pleases.

The boy, too, when he is of age to do any work, is kept busily engaged. But in the family of a peasant the work, though continuous, is not hard, and is all performed in the open air. The boys of the artisan are in much worse case. The theory of hereditary

No. 22

A TROUPE OF NAUTCH-GIRLS (p. 187)

occupations insists that he shall make an early start in his father's trade, and you will see boys who are obviously hard pressed by work in trades which demand acuteness of eyesight. The embroiderer, the wood-carver, and other craftsmen of this kind get much of the finer work done by lads, and in Delhi they are kept painting the little miniatures on ivory, which are triumphs of mechanical skill, until their sight gets weakened, and they have to take to some other occupation before they have reached manhood.

Passing on to amusements. All the village amusements are those which the people themselves provide. It is seldom that a professional troupe of acrobats, dancers, or snake-charmers finds it worth their while to give a performance in a country village. In most of these there is a sort of arena where in the evening the youths contend in wrestling, single-stick, or similar trials of skill before an applauding audience of the older men. It is only among the people of the hills that public dancing of girls and youths is to be seen, and this is generally a performance celebrated at the great agricultural festivals to promote the fertility of the soil and the ripening of the crops. Among the people of the plains dancing is confined to the troupes of professional Nautch girls, and no respectable villager, Hindu or Mohammedan, would dream of allowing his women-folk to perform in public.

The persistence of habit in the games of children is illustrated by Mr. J. Cockburn's account of his finding in the wild jungles of Mirzapur a magnificent specimen of a neolithic ring-stone which a young savage had mounted on a stick for use as a mace. In the same way in this part of the country the curious cup-shaped markings on boulders, which are a standing puzzle to archæologists, and the grooves which were originally used for sharpening the diorite celts so common along the Vindhyan hills, are now imitated by boys, in all probability lineally descended from ancestors who in comparatively modern times were still in the Age of Stone.

The mind of the child is, in fact, much the same all the world over, and uses the same playthings in the same way. Thus we find in various parts of Northern India the familiar game of Tip-cat. This is known in the hills of Kumaun under the names of Atali or Bed. The boys go into a field, and dig a hole about three inches deep in which they fix a piece of wood about a span in length, the end of which projects a short distance over the edge of the hole. Each boy in succession flings a stick at it, and he who in a given number of strokes makes it fly the greatest distance is the winner. In a more elaborate form, under the name of Gadi, it is played by the Dravidians of the Vindhyan range. The boys are divided into two parties, each of which has a Gadi or Cat of its own. The two sides sit in rows facing each other, and those who are out rest their Gadi against a brick. The side which is in strikes its Gadi with a stick to hit the Gadi of the other side. A miss puts the side out, and the others go in. The game is won when there are seven hits in succession.

Something of the nature of Prisoners' Base is played

in various ways. The boys divide into two parties, and by guessing the contents of the hand of one of the leaders are divided into 'ins' and 'outs,' or as they call themselves, 'bankers' and 'thieves.' The 'bankers' grouped behind their leader, the most powerful and active of the gang, defend their citadel, which is marked off by a line. One of the 'thieves' invades this area, and endeavours to capture a defender. But as he enters the hostile territory he must continue to shout out a series of verses describing how a wolf attacks a party of children and tries to seize them. Should he cease shouting the rhyme or be captured himself, he becomes 'dead,' and takes no further part in the game, which is carried on in succession by other members of his side until they are all 'dead,' or have succeeded in capturing all their opponents.

In the Punjab the game is played in much the same way. The parties take their places on opposite sides of a line, and one rushes out and touches an opponent and tries to get back without drawing breath, which is shown by his shouting all the time 'Kavaddi,' from which the game takes its name. If he gets back in one breath the opponent he has touched is 'dead'; but if he is caught and held until forced to draw breath, he is counted 'dead,' and goes out until the game is ended or there is an exchange of prisoners.

Another game of the same kind is called 'Dom Crow' after the scavenger tribe of that name. Each boy in turn is abused as the 'Dom,' and he rushes away and mounts a pile of sticks or cow-dung fuel cakes, shouting out 'Raja above and Doms below!' while the others try to drag him down. Whoever succeeds in maintaining his position wins.

Leap-frog in its usual form seems to be unknown, but they have a guessing game in Behar called 'Tilai Tilwa,' in which one side asks the other a question like this: 'There is a family whose house faces east and contains two males and three females. Name it.' If the leader of the gang fails to name the house, his side has to carry their opponents on their backs to that house in the village which answers the conditions, and keep them so mounted till the women of that house plead for their release.

Blind-man's Buff, known as 'Ankh Mundaul,' is a favourite game of little children. One boy is selected to be blind, and faces a wall. The others hide, and while he seeks for them, try to touch the wall. Any one who is touched by the blind man becomes a 'thief' in his stead. Bengalis, like the Italians, call the game Kāna Māchi, 'Blind Fly' and, as with us, the blind man has to touch one of the players sitting round, and after feeling him has to state his name.

Punjabi boys play games with more zest than those of other provinces. Most of their games are based on the division of the players into two parties. One method of fixing the sides is that all the boys pair off in twos, and each pair agrees to call themselves by a fancy name—'Sun and Moon,' 'Tiger and Leopard,' and so on. Presenting themselves before the two captains, each pair asks: 'Will you have Sun or Moon?' and as he answers, the division is made. When they toss for the right to begin, one captain asks the other : 'Right or Wrong?' and after the other has replied he kicks one of his slippers into the air, and the decision depends on whether it falls sole upwards or the reverse.

Tip-cat and Prisoners' Base, a game played with bat and ball, which may be cricket in a primitive stage, jumping and Hop-scotch are the favourite amusements of little Punjabi boys, while mere babies make mud pies, build houses with potsherds, or torture puppies quite like civilised children. As for toys, tops are most approved, of which the peg-top, humming-top and teetotum are the favourite varieties.

The village youths are too tired after hard field-work in the hot and cold seasons to do much in the way of amusing themselves in the short Indian twilight. But in the rains they practise various feats of skill, while the men look on and applaud the victor or jeer at the loser. One player walks backwards and strikes another who follows him on the breast with his open hand, which the other tries to catch. Or two young fellows interlock their fingers, and one tries to wrench the other's wrist. Or they place their elbows on a board, grasp wrists, and one tries to bring down the other's hand. In the eastern Punjab Saunchi is the favourite test of strength. Two young men pair off; one seizes the other by the chest, and the other tries to grasp and hold his opponent's wrist. If the striker manages to get in three blows without having his arm seized, he wins. The other wins if he can seize his opponent's arm. The struggle is often a severe test of strength and endurance, as the players in the contest of one to hold and the other to escape roll over each other on the ground time after time.

Gulli Danda, so popular with Bengalis, is said by them to be the most elementary form of cricket. But it needs some imagination to trace the resemblance. To begin with, no runs are made, and the object is merely to tire out the opposing side. The Danda or stick is about fifteen inches long, and the Gulli, pointed at both ends, is two inches or so in length. The players divide into two 'elevens,' and toss for innings. The Gulli is placed in a shallow hole, and the side which 'fields' stands in a row opposite it. The 'in' player strikes the Gulli out of the hole with his Danda, and if any of his opponents catch it, he is 'out.' The player who misses a catch is dead, but he can come to life again by making a catch.

Little girls have many games of their own, but they marry so early, and any frivolity after marriage is so strongly discouraged, that their time for amusement is soon over. After they have passed babyhood most of their games are dramatic or imitative, and all are closely connected with religion or with some ceremony. They are often accompanied by songs or some form of recitative, the words of which are unintelligible to the actors themselves. These resemble the Mantra or mystical formulæ which are the usual accompaniment of the prayers which the Hindu recites in his morning and evening devotions, when he visits the temples of the gods, or performs the rites of family life. Hence it has been conjectured with some amount of probability that many of these village games are worn-down

No. 23

Her First Lesson in Spinning (p. 166)

survivals of magical rites, such as those intended to promote the fertility of the crops. This would account for the many games which imitate marriage rites. High-caste girls with their dolls represent the union of Siva and Gauri; those of low caste that of one of the minor village deities. Many of their games, again, are little dramas based on some legend or folk-tale. Thus they imitate their elders in swinging the infant Krishna in the rainy season. Sometimes they perform what is possibly the survival of a rain charm. They go to a tank, worship the god of rain, and then divide into two parties, one girl representing the bride and another the bridegroom. The pair walk round a sacred tree in the way prescribed by the marriage ritual, while the friends of the bride jeer at the bridegroom and the others at the bride—abuse being here, as in many other cases, a mode of avoiding ill-luck. We may compare these rites with the periodical celebrations by the Dravidian tribes of the marriage of the Earth goddess and her consort, whose union year after year is supposed to promote the fertility of the soil and the ripening of the harvest.

The life of the girl's doll ends in a tragical way. It is made the subject of a rite savouring of white Magic. Once a year they are taken to the river-bank, and the owner lets them float away in the stream while the lads of the village beat them with rods. The rite is in some obscure way connected with snake-worship, and it would seem that the dolls are flung into the water and beaten by the boys as a form of expiatory offering impersonating the ill-luck of the village which is thus periodically expelled.

CHAPTER X

THE BIRTH RITES

The theory of Taboo. Hindu ceremonies. Taboos of mother and child. The birth rite. The rite of the sixth day. Protection of mother and child. The naming rite. The initiation. The doctrine of metempsychosis. Mohammedan ceremonies. Rules enforced during eclipses. Precautions to avoid the Evil Eye. The naming rite. The circumcision.

THE life of a Hindu, and in a less degree that of a Mohammedan, is regulated by a code of ritual observances, which are the chief part of his religion. These observances are intended to counteract taboo, the effects of which appear throughout the whole course of his existence. Taboo depends upon the potentiality or atmosphere which inheres in and surrounds every personality. 'Our words sanctity, pollution, infection,' to quote a recent address by Mr. E. S. Hartland, 'feebly and partially translate the intuitive dread of this potentiality which is embodied in a taboo.' This potentiality exhibits itself most vividly at the main crises of life. The mother at the time of her delivery, her child, the bride and bridegroom, the dying man, the corpse, all are specially endowed with it.

Taboo, again, is infectious; that is to say, it communicates itself freely to all those in its vicinity, and hence special precautions must be taken to obviate the dangers which may result at such times to the other members of the household, their friends, their neighbours. Further, the person in a state of taboo is particularly liable to the dangerous influences which may arise from the potentiality of those with whom he or she may come in contact. Such people are, for instance, particularly exposed to the Evil Eye. Hence the isolation enforced in the case of the person under taboo is intended not only to protect his relations from the dreaded influences which proceed from him, but also to guard him from similar dangerous effects proceeding from strangers.

These two principles will help to explain many of the obscure and tedious rites which are performed at birth, marriage, and death. They also throw some light on the view which the native of India takes of his social life. In his eyes every stranger is potentially an enemy, and hence it is needful that for the purpose of self-defence he should belong to a tribe or caste, a circle of kindred allied by blood, capable of protecting itself from the dangers of the outer world. This dangerous influence from abroad is specially manifested in the matter of food which is particularly liable to this kind of infection. It is therefore necessary that a Hindu should cook his own food, or have it cooked by some woman of his own household, on a hearth carefully guarded against pollution from outside. As we have already seen, it is only food in which the products of the sacred cow form a part which is safe from danger of this kind.

Among high-caste Hindus a woman is regarded as in a state of taboo when the first signs of pregnancy appear, and a series of rites which provide for the ceremonial parting of her hair, a favourite haunt of malignant spirits, are performed during the fourth, sixth, or eighth month before her child is born. She is at the same time forbidden to expose herself rashly in public during this period lest she may be attacked by the Evil Eye of some malevolent stranger, and when she does venture abroad she must be protected by special charms and amulets. The relations are feasted, rice and fruits, emblems of fertility, are poured into her lap, and a rite is performed with the object of ensuring that the expected child will be a boy.

When the time of delivery approaches, the expectant mother is carefully isolated in a room or shed attached to the house. Here she is attended by the wife of the village Chamār, or currier, who acts as midwife, to be succeeded after a few days by the wife of the barber. Fortunately cases of difficult parturition seldom occur. In such cases the woman is at the mercy of an ignorant, untrained assistant, and permanent injury to her health occurs. This danger has now to some small extent been obviated by the establishment of female hospitals in the larger cities. The birth is announced by the firing of guns from the house-top, the noise of which scares any evil spirits which may be skulking in the neighbourhood. The period of seclusion of mother and infant varies with the caste, some of those of higher rank keeping her imprisoned for at least fifteen days, while among those of a lower grade she simply bathes and rejoins her family almost immediately after the birth.

Among those castes which follow Brahmanical rules, after the child is born the first birth rite is performed. The father bathes, offers prayers to the god Ganesa, patron of good-luck and remover of obstacles, imploring him that the child may be good, strong, and wise; that, if she has become specially impure by violating any of the prescribed rules of conduct or food, the mother's sin may be forgiven, and that its consequences may not be visited upon the baby. He then invokes the sainted ancestors of his family and the nine planets which preside over domestic rites. With a golden skewer or the third finger of his right hand he smears the tongue of the child with a mixture of butter and honey, while a prayer is recited asking that the child may be endowed with all material blessings. The father then takes the child in his arms, and touching each member of its body while reciting the suitable formulæ, prays that they may be endowed with strength. Finally, the father is purified by asperging him with holy water sprinkled from a brush made of sacred grass. The husband thus joins in the taboo which surrounds his wife, a belief which is probably at the root of the curious custom of the Couvade.

This is followed on the sixth day after birth by a remarkable rite in which the Hindu unwittingly accepts the conclusions of our modern pathologists. This is the usual time at which infantile lockjaw, the result of the neglect of sanitary precautions at birth, usually appears, and is exceedingly fatal to Indian babies. The sixth day is therefore deified under the name of Shashthi, who is regarded as the goddess presiding over it. A place is carefully purified, and the image of the deity being drawn upon a piece of wood, she is solemnly invoked, invited to be present, installed, and worshipped with the appropriate formulæ and offerings.

During the period of seclusion mother and child are carefully protected. The dangers to which they are exposed are impersonated in a band of birth fiends who beset the room in which they rest. In Behar the fiend takes the shape of a night-bird which sucks the blood of any one whose name it hears. Hence, after sunset no one dares to address mother or child by name. Or, as among the Oraons, it may come in the form of a cat which tears the mother's womb, or as a hen which scratches her with its claws. Various devices are employed to scare such demons. Especially on the sixth day after birth the women of the house sit up all night and watch, beat drums, sing, and talk to scare the fiend. Others surround the mother's bed with a fishing-net or with the coils of a jungle creeper, place an iron knife or scythe beneath it, and an iron pot at the door, the virtues of 'cauld iron' being everywhere recognised. But the most valued precaution is to keep a fire constantly burning in the delivery room. Should it go out the fiend will enter, tread on the cold ashes, and make its dreaded mark on the forehead of the baby. These devices, effective though they may be for repelling evil spirits, are most injurious to mother and child, particularly in the hot season. But considerations of health must always yield to the sense of spirit danger.

After the taboo is removed and the mother and her child resume family life, two special rites are performed, one to provide the baby with a name, the second to introduce it formally into the circle of its caste.

As is the case with all people in the lower culture, the name is an important part of the personality. It is selected on various grounds—either as a recognition that the child is really an ancestor reborn in the family, his name being assigned to it; or it may be the name of a god or goddess, through whose aid in answer to prayer or vow the child was granted, and under whose protection it is solemnly placed. Among the forest tribes it is often that of the sacred tree beneath whose shade the child was born. In any case, the name is a sacred portion of the infant's being, and to ensure that it may not be communicated to some malevolent stranger who may work evil by its means, one name is conferred for everyday use, while another is whispered in the child's ear, and by it no one dares to address it. In high-caste families the god Ganesa is again invoked as a protector, and is propitiated by an offering of the five products of the cow. On this day for the first time the child is allowed to see the sun, and he is made to plant his foot on a coin while the gods are invoked to grant that he may be rich enough in after life to regard money as the very dust beneath his feet.

When the name has been thus bestowed, the next rite is a species of initiation by which the baby becomes duly introduced into the caste circle of its parents. Up to this time the child is hardly regarded as possessing a sentient soul, and he is subject to no restrictions in regard to food or drink. When he is once initiated his real life as a Hindu begins. This rite assumes various forms. It is sometimes represented by the solemn feeding of the child on sacred rice and other substances each of which is supposed to impart some special quality. This is usually combined with a general feast to the members of the commensal circle, which the Romans called Confarreatio, from which important results are believed to follow. The boy being now free to eat and drink within his group, and strictly forbidden to share in the food of those who are strangers to it, becomes united to his clansmen by an indissoluble bond. In popular opinion taboo, or impurity from outside, is usually communicated through food, and no one eating with his clansmen is likely to practise magical acts to their detriment by means of the common meal.

Among Brahmans and those who follow their rule of life, this is further supplemented by a special act of initiation. Before this is performed the boy is purified by undergoing a ceremonial tonsure which finally rids him of any of the pollution acquired at birth which may still cling to him. His ears are then bored to receive the rings which through life will guard him against the effects of taboo impersonated in the demons and evil spirits which ever beset his path. These preliminary rites of purification, directed against spiritual rather than physical pollution, prepare him for the final ceremony of initiation. This consists in the girding of the boy with the sacred cord which marks his status as one of the twice-born castes. This constitutes, as it were, a sacred circle which envelops his body, and within which no evil influence from abroad can penetrate. The thread itself is valueless as a protective until it has been sanctified by the blessing of Brahmans and the recital of texts from the sacred books. From this time the boy's spiritual life begins; he is taught to recite the famous Vedic prayer to the Sun god, and he is now ripe to begin his religious education and to share in the privileges of his brethren.

It will have been noticed that this rite of initiation is performed for boys alone. A girl, in the Hindu view, needs no initiation in childhood. This is deferred until by virtue of the marriage rite she is severed from her own relations and is formally introduced into a new circle of kindred, that of her husband.

Before leaving the incidents of childhood, it may be remarked that many of the beliefs regarding children are based on the doctrine of metempsychosis or rebirth, which is one of the foundations of the Hindu faith. According to this theory, life is continuous from one generation to another, and the soul is subject to a series of births, as gods or men, plants, stones, or animals (for the theory of Animism fixes no bounds to the universal presence of spirit in all the forms of creation), until at length it becomes fitted to be reabsorbed into the self-existent Spirit of the Universe.

From this follow certain inevitable deductions. The first is illustrated by numerous cases in Indian criminal records, where the ceremonial killing of a male child has been performed as a cure for barrenness, the theory being that the soul of the murdered boy becomes reincarnated in the woman, who performs the rite with a desire to secure offspring. Usually she effects union with the spirit of the child by bathing over its body or in the water in which the corpse has been washed. Cases have recently occurred in which the woman actually bathed in the blood of the child. Some Punjabi women, when cursed, as they imagine, by the birth of a girl, take the child to the jungle and expose it with the invocation: 'Don't come back, but send a brother!' On returning to the place next day, if the mother finds that the dogs or jackals have dragged the child towards her house, she infers that another girl will be born. If it is dragged away from the house, she rejoices, saying: 'A brother will come!'

Again, when a child dies it is usually buried under the house threshold, in the belief that as the parents tread daily over its grave, its soul will be reborn in the family. Here, as Mr. Rose suggests, we reach an explanation of the rule that children of Hindus are buried, not cremated. Their souls do not pass into the ether with the smoke of the pyre, but remain on earth to be reincarnated in the household. Hence, too, the high regard for a first-born son, who is supposed to be the spirit of his father reborn, some Punjab tribes going so far as to believe that the father actually dies at his birth. This also accounts for the ill omen attaching to a first-born girl, whom some castes, until the practice was stopped by British law, were in the habit of destroying.

The Mohammedans in their birth and other family customs have adopted many practices not sanctioned in the law of the Prophet. They desire male offspring as much as the Hindus, but not, of course, from the same religious motive. To secure an heir women appeal to saints, living or dead, and have recourse to many kinds of charms. Some, learned in the art of magic, give them pieces of sugar on which the mystic titles of Allah have been blown, or written charms to be washed and the infusion drunk or used in the bath once a month. Some saints are noted as givers of children, like Salīm Chishti at Fatehpur-Sikri, near Agra, and to acquire his favour a rag is tied by childless women to the delicate marble tracery of his tomb, thus bringing them into direct communion with the spirit of the holy man. Like the Hindu woman, the Musalmāni wears a piece of iron in her dress and a 'spirit-laden' cord round her waist. She is subject to various taboos. She must not go under the canopy erected at marriages or feasts; she must avoid marriage and death rites; she must not pass under the city gates, nor cross a river or sea—all places which are the haunt of spirits. During an eclipse, when a demon is eating the moon, neither she nor her relatives must eat, drink, smoke, cut or break anything because spirits are about. If she eats betel-leaf, her child will be born with ears folded like it; if she cuts anything, the baby will have a deformed finger or a hare-lip. In the final days of pregnancy she must lay aside her new clothes and jewellery, never colour her feet and hands with henna, nor darken her teeth with Missi powder. Special vows are made to ensure easy delivery and the safety of the child, and a special rite is performed by which the sex of the expected infant may be divined.

When the child is born, if it be a boy, the midwife, in order to baffle the Evil Eye, announces that it is a one-eyed girl. If it be a girl, the fact is stated at once, because the female sex is safe from fascination. For the same reason a boy-baby is dressed in dirty clothes or in a girl's dress. Frankincense and mustard are burnt, and the smoke waved over mother and child to scare evil spirits.

The naming of the child is the occasion of a feast. The name is selected sometimes by opening the Korān at a venture, and the first letter of the first word in the third line of the page is the initial of the name. Sometimes a name is chosen which was borne by some ancestor, or because it is considered lucky, or because it has some religious significance. The period of the mother's seclusion ends on the fortieth day. Next comes the rite of salt tasting, a form of *confarreatio*, which is done when the baby is able to take any food stronger than milk. This is followed, in the fourth or fifth year, by a formal initiation, when a feast is given, and the child is made to recite, after the priest, the opening chapter of the Korān. The final ceremony of initiation to religious privileges is that of circumcision, which resembles that of the Jews, but is simpler and less painful. The boy then joins in the observance of the first Ramzān feast, and in the dinner which follows. Thus childhood ends, and the boy is ready to undertake the responsibilities of married life.

CHAPTER XI

THE MARRIAGE RITES

The prohibited degrees. The horoscope. The matchmaker. Survivals of primitive forms of marriage. Marriage by purchase. Widow marriage. The marriage ritual among the forest tribes: among Brahmans, artisans and traders: among Mohammedans.

MARRIAGE, as we have seen, contemplates that the parties are under the influence of taboo, and the rites are intended to obviate its dangers, and in particular those which may prevent the union from being fertile.

An elaborate series of rules prescribes the prohibited degrees. Among the Dravidians there are exogamous divisions of the tribe which depend upon totemism, each bearing the name of a tree, animal, or some material object, which the members of the sept regard with respect. Even among castes in a higher grade, like the Kumhār potters of Orissa, we find sections named after the tiger, the weasel, or the snake. But while no man may marry within his own section, the name of it goes only in the male side, and consequently, so far as the rule of exogamy is concerned, there is nothing to prevent him from marrying near relations on the female side. To avoid this, marriage with any person descended in direct succession from the same parents is forbidden. Different castes, however, interpret the rules in different ways, some, like the Santāls, inclining to laxity, and while prohibiting intermarriage with relatives on the father's side, allowing very near alliances with the kindred of the mother. On the other hand, the menial castes of the plains generally forbid intermarriage so long as any relationship, however remote, can be traced between the parties.

When we pass from the menial castes to the Brahmans we find a different state of things. They are divided into eponymous sections, Gotras, 'cow-pens,' as they are called, each of which is exogamous. Here, as among the menial castes, relationship is traced in the male line, and it has become necessary to form an elaborate table of prohibited degrees.

Further than this, no pair can be married unless the horoscopes agree. This is a matter of negotiation between the astrologers on both sides, who represent their clients as our family solicitors do. In Bengal the arrangements for a wedding are made by a professional match-maker, the Ghātak, a fussy, gossiping, self-important official, who considers the failure of a match which he has undertaken to arrange an insult to himself. To the west his place is taken by the barber, who here, as elsewhere, is a scandal-monger, fond of meddling with the affairs of other people.

It is unnecessary to discuss at length the survivals of primitive forms of marriage. Polyandry prevails throughout the Himālayan area from Kashmir to

Assam, and some tribes continue to trace descent in the female line, and give the maternal uncle a leading place in the ceremonial. Some cases of feigned resistance by the friends of the bride directed against the bridegroom may have come down from the days of capture marriage; but many of these mock combats are more probably intended to scare evil spirits. We have seen that the bride is admitted to her new kindred by the common meal. A cruder method of securing the same result is by means of the blood covenant, each of the pair being smeared with the blood of the other. This custom still survives among some castes in Bengal, but in other places it has been superseded by the rite of rubbing the forehead of the bride with vermilion. There are also survivals of the curious habit of marrying the pair to trees, the purpose of which is still uncertain.

Usages such as these, interesting though they may be as throwing light upon the evolution of society, are now of little practical importance, because we find that they have been generally replaced by so-called marriage by purchase. In these commercial days, of course, everything, including brides and bridegrooms, has its price. But originally the gifts at marriage were tokens of a solemn pledge, a part of one's self given to another and received in return from him as a mode ratifying the contract. At the present time the practice is not uniform, in some cases the bride's father, in others that of the bridegroom, paying a price. It depends, in fact, upon demand and supply. Castes, for instance, which allow widow marriage get their brides cheap; in those which follow the law of hypergamy bridegrooms are dear.

Among the hill tribes who cannot afford to purchase, the custom of what is called Beena marriage is common. The bridegroom serves for his wife as Jacob did for Rachel. Some tribes, while the youth is undergoing his period of probation, carefully exclude him from the society of his future bride. In others no restriction is enforced. In short, among many of these tribes it is hard to decide whether marriage, in our sense of the term, exists. Among the Nāgas and their kindred the intercourse of the sexes is practically unrestricted, and cohabitation implies marriage.

Widow marriage, again, regulates caste precedence. The higher castes do not permit it, while it is common among those of lower rank. It is therefore supposed to involve discredit, and is not attended by the rites which sanctify a regular marriage, but is done secretly at night, and the only formality is the feast which signifies that it is approved by the brethren.

We may take as an example of the marriage ritual that of the Majhwārs, a Dravidian tribe of the central hills. The negotiations are begun by the Patāri, or tribal priest. When he has selected the bride, the friends of the boy visit her and make a careful examination, to make sure that she has no mental or bodily defect. Assured of this, they make a second visit, bringing with them a supply of cakes. The clansmen of the bride are assembled, and the fathers exchange cups of spirits, addressing each other as connections by marriage. The remainder of the food and liquor is consumed by the clansmen, who thus authenticate the betrothal. After this the maternal uncles on both sides provide presents for their relatives.

Then follows the wedding. As the youth starts to fetch his bride, his mother waves over his head a rice-pounder and a tray containing a lighted lamp in order to scare away evil spirits. He is carried in a litter, and when the party reach the bride's village they halt on the outskirts, while the boy's father sends in advance a present of jewels for the bride, which she wears at the marriage rite.

This takes place in a shed built of bamboos, with posts made from the tribal sacred tree. The first pole is planted by the Baiga, or medicine-man, Brahmans having no place in the rite except when in the higher families they are consulted to fix an auspicious time. The husband of the boy's sister acts as best man, lifts him out of his litter, and provides him with a special amulet against the Evil Eye. Meanwhile the tribal priest makes in the courtyard a sacred square with lines of barley-flour, thus protecting it from evil magic, and in the centre of this the bride's father solemnly plants a spear. The best man escorts the boy into this enclosure, waving a fan to scare the spirits which may be hovering about his head. Here the female relations of the bride bar his progress, and will not admit him until they receive a present.

The bride is then brought out from an inner room, and she and the bridegroom sit facing the east on coarse mats made of leaves of the Sāl (*Shorea robusta*), which is held sacred by the tribe. The best man knots

No. 24

A Peasant's Hut, Bengal (p. 127)

together the garments of the pair, enclosing in the knot a copper coin and a piece of betel-nut, while the tribal priest makes the pair move slowly round the spear five times, following the course of the sun, the bridegroom walking in advance of the bride, who rests her hands on his shoulders. Then comes the giving away of the bride, which is done by her father, and the gift is accepted by the father of the boy. They are then seated on mats, spirits are poured into the cups of each, and these they interchange and taste. The mother or grandmother of the bride washes the feet of the pair, and marks their foreheads with a mixture of curds and rice, after which the bridegroom smears the nose, forehead, and hair-parting of the girl with vermilion. This is the binding portion of the rite, after which they eat out of the same dish.

Next day a feast is provided for the kinsmen. But the bridegroom and his best man refuse to share in it until they receive a present.

After this the bride, if she be nubile, which is usually the case, is taken home by her husband. When they arrive at his house, a sort of supplementary marriage rite is performed, and as a special means of securing fertility to the union, the women bring lucky earth from the village tank, seat the pair upon it, bathe and anoint them with oil and turmeric, after which presents are interchanged. After this, magical charms are done. A measure is filled with rice, and the contents are poured over the heads of the pair. The rice is collected and replaced in the measure, and if it overflows the edges, which it is always arranged shall happen, the marriage will certainly be prosperous. When all is over, the boy's father addresses the assembled clansmen: 'I have done my duty by getting them married. Let them now work for their living. If they respect me, let them give me a drink of water in my old age.'

This is the marriage rite in its simplest form. It has been elaborated by the Brahmans into a tedious ceremony, many of the observances being puerile and lasting over several days. But in all its forms the principles are identical. The chief difference between the simpler and the more elaborate forms of the ceremony is that in the former the bride usually begins married life at once; in the latter it is postponed until she comes of age. The rites of the agricultural and artisan castes are a compound of the higher and the lower forms.

The rules regulating marriage connections between Mohammedans are much simpler than among Hindus. Consanguinity, affinity, fosterage, are bars to union. No marriage can be performed between the ascendants and descendants of a single ancestor, with paternal or maternal uncles or aunts. On the other hand, the marriage of cousins is recognised and even encouraged. Infant marriage is unknown except among those castes with Hindu affinities, and there is no prejudice against widow marriage. This and the wider range of food which is permitted to Mohammedans largely account for the great increase among them in parts of Northern India, especially in Bengal.

The Indian Mohammedans have adopted many of the superstitious Hindu beliefs. The bride is regarded as taboo and exposed to the attacks of evil spirits. In Western India, after the betrothal, a line of earthen pots containing food is arranged for the refreshment of the ancestral spirits of the family. With the object of repelling demons, the bride and bridegroom are anointed with a mixture of wheat and pulse flour, turmeric and sesamum oil. The handmill in which these grains are ground has its handle smeared with sandal-wood paste, and nuts, betel, and other fruits wrapped in a red cloth are tied to it. Then seven women who have never lost a husband grind the flour for the anointing, which thus becomes a longevity charm. Rice is thrown over the heads of the pair; a woman passes sesamum seed seven times round them, and by cracking her finger joints across her temples takes on herself any ill-luck which may menace them. A dagger or other iron implement and a lemon are handed to them, which they must keep till the bath on the wedding-day. A gold bracelet must also be worn during this period as a protective.

When the bridegroom comes to fetch the bride, he wears the Sehra, or flower-chaplet, as a talisman. As he passes under her window the bride showers rice over him. He is received in the hall, in which three seats are placed—one for the bridegroom, the second for the representative of the bride, the third for the Kāzi, or registrar. The Kāzi asks the bride's agent whether he accepts the youth as her husband with a certain dowry. The bridegroom, after reciting the Mohammedan creed, is asked the same question, and after assent is given the Kāzi formally records the proceedings, and the guests, raising their hands, offer the thanksgiving. Meanwhile, music and singing go on until the bridegroom is led into the women's apartments. On his way in he is guarded by his sisters or other near relations from the assaults of the younger sisters or connections of the girl, who, if they get a chance, wring his ears unmercifully. After this the bride, veiled and arrayed in her marriage dress and jewellery, is led in and seated before her husband. A humorous performance of the rite of eating together follows. The bride, who should not move a muscle, is helped by one of the party to take a piece of sugar-candy, cake, or a dry date. Her hand is stretched out to her husband's mouth, and as he tries to secure the morsel, it is snatched away. Merriment of this kind goes on all night, until at dawn the youth for the first time is shown the girl's face in a mirror, and from a Korān placed between them the Chapter of Peace is read. Then he lifts her in his arms, conducts her to her litter, and conveys her home.

CHAPTER XII

DEATH RITES

Various modes of disposal of the dead. Burial and cremation. Exposure to wild beasts. Platform burial. Burial in its rudest form. Crouched burial. Niche burial. Burial of those under taboo. The Srāddha. Rites of the Mohammedans.

THE chief methods of disposal of the dead are cremation and earth burial, the former prevailing among all the tribes which follow Aryan usage, the latter among the menial castes. Methods differing from these are found only on the outskirts of Northern India. The Nāga tribes of Assam expose the corpse on a platform, from which the bones are subsequently removed and stored in an ossuary. Some of them, however, bury their dead and perform a remarkable rite at the grave. After it is filled in, large stones are piled upon it, and the men, dressed in their war-dress, shout and cry: 'What spirit has killed our friend? Where have you fled? If we could see you we would slay you with the spear.' Then with a war-whoop they curse the evil spirit and beat the grave with their weapons.

There are, again, aberrant forms of burial. Among the wildest tribes the corpse is merely flung into a ravine or some cleft of the rocks, and stones are piled over it to prevent the ghost from 'walking.' The same result is attained by some of the menial tribes who bury the dead face downwards and fill the grave with thorns. In other cases, possibly with the same intention, the corpse is bound with cords or interred in the crouched position. Mohammedans make, as we shall see, special arrangements to prepare the dead man for the judgment day. Persons under taboo, such as women dying in a state of pollution or in childbirth, are buried, the idea being that they are likely to turn into dangerous ghosts unless their bodies are kept near at hand and rites of propitiation performed. Many of the lower castes merely singe the face of the corpse and consign it to a river, and this is done with the bones of the cremated dead.

When an orthodox Hindu is at the point of death, a Brahman brings a cow, marks its forehead with vermilion, and salutes it. A little Ganges water is poured into the mouth of the dying man; alms are given to Brahmans and to beggars; and just at the moment of dissolution he is removed into the open air or conveyed to the river-bank. The object is, first, that the house may be free from the death pollution; secondly, that in the open air the soul may have free exit from the body; and thirdly, that resting on the ground or in a holy place, it may be safe from the attacks of evil spirits. Such spirits cannot rest upon the ground. Hence, when the bones are being taken to the Ganges, the jar which contains them is hung on a tree where no demons have access, and the soul may visit them if so disposed.

When death occurs and the wailing is going on, the chief mourner bathes and shaves his moustache and head to free himself from pollution. Balls of rice are laid near the corpse for the refreshment of the spirit; the corpse is washed and shrouded. If the dead man has left a widow, she is led away by the old women, who strip off her bodice, break the bangles on her wrists, tear off her jewellery, and shave her head. Henceforth she lives a life of degradation, dresses only in white, and acts as the household drudge, because she is considered to have incurred the wrath of the gods.

The corpse is laid upon a bier and carried away feet foremost so that the ghost may not find its way back to the house. The chief mourner follows the bier, holding a pot full of burning ashes, and the second mourner scatters food along the road to propitiate evil spirits. No women join the funeral. In Western India, the customs of which are described generally here, one of the mourners, when they approach the place of cremation, picks up a stone, known as the 'life stone,' which is supposed to be a refuge for the ghost, and to which food is offered.

When they arrive at the burning ground the holy fire is kindled, but in the Ganges valley it is provided by a Dom. The pyre is prepared and the corpse is laid on it with its head facing the Himālaya. Butter is dropped into the mouth, eyes, nose, and ears, and balls of flour are placed around. When all is ready the chief mourner walks round the pyre in the course of the sun and sets fire to it. When the skull bursts, the mourner pours water upon it to cool the ghost. The final act is the collection of the bone fragments, which is usually done on the fourth day. They are enclosed in a jar, which is buried until an opportunity occurs of sending them to the river.

The Hindu believes that when the soul leaves the body it assumes the shape of a little, feeble mannikin, exposed to injuries of all kinds. In order to protect it, it is necessary to furnish it with a sort of intermediate body, interposed, as it were, between the gross body which has been destroyed by fire and the new body which under the law of metempsychosis it will by and by assume. If it be not furnished with this intermediate body it will wander about in the form of a Preta or evil spirit.

The rites by which this new body is prepared are known as Srāddha. During this time, which usually lasts ten days, the mourners are under strict taboo. Except for the purpose of visiting the cremation ground, their chief never leaves the house. Leaves are used at meals in place of metal dishes; they neither buy food nor cook it, eating only fish, herbs, and other things supplied by their friends. They neither pray nor worship the gods; the husband sleeps apart from his wife on a blanket, mat, or on the bare ground. Day by day offerings of balls of flour are made by which each member of the new body is gradually constructed. When this is complete the clothes and other articles used by the dead man, which are regarded as infected

A Bhotiya Village in the Northern Hills, Assam (p. 126)

by the death taboo, are given to a Brahman of a low class which only accepts such gifts. Then follow bathing and purification by which the death pollution is finally removed from the house.

The soul, once admitted to the society of the Pitri, or sainted ancestors, cannot rest in peace unless it is supported by the pious care of the decendants. Hence the Srāddha, which is really based upon the necessity of feeding the soul of the dead, must be repeated at annual intervals, and the final repose of the spirit is secured by a visit to a holy place, such as Gaya in Behar or Benares. Here, under the guidance of a Brahman, the mourner makes a little pile of sand to serve as an altar. Food for the spirit is laid around it, water is poured to refresh the thirsty soul, and a lamp is lighted to guide it to the feast. As in the original Srāddha, Brahmans are fed, and the food given to them passes to the spirit. After a year or two, when the recollection of the dead ceases to affect the mourners, it is assumed that the uneasy spirit has finally gained its rest, and the rites are discontinued. But at each successive death in the family the sainted dead are commemorated, invited to attend the funeral feast, and are refreshed by the periodical feeding of Brahmans.

The elaborate ceremonial which attends the Hindu death rites are wanting in those of the Mahommedans. When death is near, that chapter of the Korān which speaks of death and the Paradise which awaits the true believer is recited in the ear of the dying man, and a few drops of honey are poured into his mouth that he may not be tempted to taste the dainties offered to him in the death agony by the fiend who lies in wait for his departing soul. After death the mouth and eyes are closed, the corpse is bathed, perfumed, and carefully shrouded. If the death occurs at night nothing more is done till the morning. Otherwise the corpse is placed at once upon the bier, which is borne by friends who insist on sharing in this pious duty, and with cries, 'There is no God but Allah!' is carried to the cemetery. If there be a mosque close by it is laid in the outer court. The mourners wash and join in the funeral prayer. Then they move to the grave and lay the body within it, the head to the north and the body leaning to the right side, so that the face is turned towards the holy city of Mecca. Some clods of earth which have been sanctified by the recital of passages from the Korān are placed on the body or on the coffin, if one be provided, with the words from the Korān: 'Of earth We made you, to earth We return you, and will raise you at the Day of Resurrection.'

It is believed that the dead man in the grave is visited by the two angels, Munkar, 'The Unknown,' and Nakīr, 'The Repudiator,' who interrogate him on his belief in the Prophet and his religion, and on his conduct in life. To prepare him for this visit special precautions are taken. When the grave is dug, a sort of side-chamber is constructed in the side facing Mecca, in which the dead man, when the angels appear, may be able to sit up and answer their questions. To assist him in this ordeal the Pathāns of the frontier place before him a tablet of stone on which the Creed is engraved, lest in his terror memory should fail him.

The mourning rites of the Mohammedans are much less stringent than those of the Hindus, from whom, however, they seem to have adopted various practices. Thus, in some families the clothes of the dead are distributed, with food, to beggars, and the death pollution is so far recognised that for two days after the funeral some families cook no food in the house of mourning, and the family are supplied by their relations. On the third day a death service is held at a mosque, at which all relatives and acquaintances attend, when passages from the Korān are read and a prayer is made that the merit of the recitation may reach the soul of the deceased. A tray containing flowers and perfumes is passed round, from which each friend takes a flower and all are poured upon the grave. This is followed by the death feast, in which the animistic idea that the soul needs food is obvious, though this is no part of the orthodox belief. These feasts should be repeated on the fortieth day, when mourning ends, in the fourth, sixth, ninth months, and on the last day of the year in which the death occurred. But it is only wealthy people who do more than a perfunctory observance of the fortieth day rite.

The only actual mourning prescribed is for the widow, who must remain in strict seclusion for four months and ten days, during which she is forbidden to marry. Like the Hindu widow, she breaks her bangles, but, unless when they are of gold or silver, she never again wears bracelets or a nose-ring, until she marries again. The actual period of mourning is fixed at six months, during which there are no feasts, gaiety, or music in the house. After this the members of the family resume their usual mode of life.

CHAPTER XIII

POPULAR RELIGION AND BELIEFS

Hinduism and Islām. Animism. The powers of Nạture: Sun, Moon, Planets, Eclipses. Rivers and springs. Mountains. Spirits of the forest. Tree-worship. The jungle Mothers. Mother Earth: her marriage. The malignant Mothers. The village gods: their shrines. Malignant spirits: the Rākshasa, the Deo, the Daitya, the Bhūt. Animal-worship: Tigers, Snakes. Totemism. Progress of Animism into Hinduism.

IT is not proposed to undertake an examination of the great historical religions of Northern India. Suffice it to say that in the three northern Provinces, Bengal, the United Provinces, and the Punjab, out of a total population of some 153 millions, about 103 millions are so-called Hindus, 46 millions Mohammedans, and the remainder includes Christians, Parsis, Jews, and other faiths of small numerical importance. But these figures must be accepted with some reservation. In the case of definite, clearly marked faiths, like those of the Christian or the Mussulman, there can be no room for doubting the correctness of the enumeration. But the term Hindu is exceedingly vague, and almost defies definition. It includes the followers of a highly philosophical system of theology, and it shelters under its wing people whose beliefs are a crude form of

Animism. An attempt was made at the last census to separate Animists from Hindus, but without much success. What was done was merely to set apart jungle tribes, like Gonds and Kols, and to call them Animists, while menials in the plains, such as Doms, whose religion is of much the same type as that of the forest folk, were enumerated as Hindus. It is, in fact, quite impossible to separate Hindus from Animists, and even the converts to Islām retain much of their primitive beliefs under a thin veneer of the creed of the Prophet.

Animism is thus the basis of the popular belief, and this chapter will be devoted to an attempt to explain its character and development.

'All the many movements and changes perpetually taking place in the world of things were,' says Dr. Jevons, 'explained by primitive man on the theory that every object which had activity enough to affect him in any way was animated by a life and will like his own.' 'It divides,' writes Professor Tylor, who invented the name, 'into two great dogmas forming part of one consistent doctrine: first, concerning souls of individual creatures capable of continued existence after the death or destruction of the body; second, concerning other spirits, upward to the rank of powerful deities. Spiritual beings are held to affect or control the events of the material world, and man's life here and hereafter; and it being considered that they hold intercourse with men, and receive pleasure or displeasure from human actions, the belief in their existence leads naturally, and it might also be said

No. 26

Ploughing (p. 158)

inevitably, sooner or later to active reverence and propitiation. Thus Animism, in its full development, includes the belief in souls and in a future state, in controlling deities and subordinate spirits, these doctrines practically resulting in some kind of active worship.'

The North Indian peasant considers that he is environed by a world of spirits which control all the conditions of his life. These spirits, as a rule, affect him more for evil than for good, and, as might be expected, those that are malignant in their nature require special propitiation, while those that are benevolent are accepted as normal, and receive only slight and infrequent worship.

In the earliest stages no attempt is made to distribute the functions of the individuals of this spirit world. This forms a later development. No clear line, again, is drawn between the various kinds of created beings and things which are animated by spirit agency. Hence shape-shifting, which with us survives only in our nursery tales, is believed by the more ignorant classes to be one of the normal incidents of life. In the same way the doctrines of metempsychosis and soul-transmigration are accepted. The boy born in the family possesses the spirit and attributes of a deceased ancestor, and the soul passes through a series of rebirths, now as a Raja, now an outcast, now an animal, now an insect, until it is finally absorbed into the World Spirit.

It is extremely difficult to make even a rough classification of vague, amorphous beliefs like these. The peasant, however, generally distinguishes between the spirits which animate the natural objects which surround him and the tribe of ghosts and spirits, not embodied in the forms of Nature, which control his life.

In the first class come those natural phenomena, the movements and peculiarities of which are supposed to be due to an indwelling spirit agency, like the powers of Nature. These are perhaps the first phenomena which attract the attention of the savage. First in order come the Sun, Moon, and the Planets.

Sun-worship is found both among the Aryan and non-Aryan races. In the latter, among the Dravidian Oraons of Bengal, he is identified with the Supreme Deity, is worshipped twice a year and also at weddings. Among the menials of the plains he is held in equal honour, worshipped on Sundays, and in Bengal, at a special festival, known as the Chat Pūja, when the people gather at a river or pool, offer oblations to the setting Sun, and repeat the rite next morning. The primitive nature of the cult is shown by the fact that no Brahmans are employed, the officiant being an elderly member of the family, usually a female. Even low-class Mohammedans share in his worship. The higher classes worship him daily when they bathe, by a recital of the Gayatri or Vedic hymn in his honour. He is regarded as a male, and is sometimes in Bengal provided with a female consort, a principle which will be further considered in connection with Earth-worship.

The Moon is a deity of a lower grade. He is believed to preside over the growth of the crops, is a healer of wounds, specially those of the eye. 'There is,' says Mr. Gait, 'a very general superstition that if any but a worshipper should happen to see the Moon on the day fixed for his worship, he will suffer a loss of reputation. To prevent worse from happening, a person who unluckily sees the Moon on such an occasion takes up five stones, and, after touching his forehead with them, throws them on his neighbour's roof. If the latter then abuses him, it is believed that atonement has been made, and that no further evil will result.'

The other planets are important chiefly from the point of view of astrology and the preparation of the horoscope, which in all well-born families regulates marriage. But the peasant takes more interest in the phenomena of eclipses, which are regarded as the work of a demon attempting to devour the Sun or Moon. He can be scared by beating of drums and execrations while the eclipse is in progress, and by pious people this is regarded as a period of taboo, when food remaining in the house becomes 'impure,' and the earthen vessels used at the time must be broken. The only way of avoiding the taboo is to place a leaf of the holy basil-tree in the jars, and to sprinkle them with Ganges water.

Rivers and springs are believed to flow under the agency of an indwelling spirit, which is generally benignant. Hence bathing brings the sinner or the man polluted by taboo into communion with this spirit, and makes him clean in the moral, rather than in the physical, sense. First of the holy rivers is the Ganges, which, like others, is specially sacred at certain auspicious conjunctions of the planets, at which times enormous crowds assemble to bathe on her banks. In Bengal goats are sacrificed on such occasions, probably to propitiate the goddess in her malignant form when she devastates the land with floods, or engulfs swimmers. These are sometimes thrown alive into the water, and are taken out by men of the boatman caste, who eat their flesh. 'Many ascetics,' writes Mr. Gait, 'perform a special penance in her honour, which consists in spending every night in the month of Māgh (January, when the cold is intense) seated on a small platform erected over the river, engaged in such prayer and meditation as their sufferings from the cold will allow.' Some places along the Ganges' banks—Hardwar, Bithur, Allahabad, Benares, and Ganga Sagar at the mouth of the Hugli, are the most sacred places in Northern India.

The other rivers are much less important from the point of view of religion, but they also have their holy places, of which the most noticeable is Muttra, on the Jumna. This river-spirit is often personified and becomes a river-god, like the mysterious Mohammedan saints, Khwāja Khizr, and Pir Badr, and Koila Bāba, 'Charcoal Father,' in Bengal, sometimes taking the form of a female, sometimes of an old, grey-bearded personage to whom the fishermen of Behar make an offering of grain and molasses when they launch a boat or cast a new net.

In the same way sacred wells abound, some adopted into the cult of, and consecrated by the legends of some of the gods or goddesses; others, which by the changing colour of their water and their periodical ebb and flow are regarded as oracular; some which have underground connection with the Ganges.

Mountains are naturally regarded with awe and are supposed to be spirit-haunted. The Himālaya, with its marvellous range of peaks crowning the horizon, inaccessible to the foot of man, was conceived to be the home of the gods. But except in this form, mountain-worship is not an important belief among the people of the plains. It is different with the Dravidian tribes of the central hills. The Mundas and allied tribes of Chota Nagpur revere a mountain-god known as Marang Buru, or in the tongue of the plains-men, Bar Pahār, 'the great mountain,' who is worshipped with animal sacrifice upon a flat rock of a hill-top, where, after feasting, the Santāls work themselves into a state of frenzy to charm the rain. The guardian goddess of the Vindhyan range dwells in a cavern where the hills approach the Ganges. Here was the famous temple of the Thugs, whose patron goddess she was, and her priests fattened on their share of the plunder of countless victims.

But the manifestations of Nature's power which we have been considering are not so closely connected with man as those which appeal to him in the course of his jungle life or in the early stages of agriculture. The vague uncanniness of the jungle, where he was constantly exposed to accident, to the attacks of wild beasts, to disease, the result of malaria, must at once have impressed his mind. Every tree seemed to him haunted by a spirit, to which was due the periodical decay of its foliage and its fresh growth in spring.

At a later stage his attention became devoted to special kinds of trees, those which produced food or intoxicants, those like the Banyan, which compel awe or admiration, those which assume uncanny forms—all the result of spirit action. Among the people of Chota Nagpur the Karam tree (*Neuclea parvifolia*) is held sacred by the Oraons, who worship it at their harvest-home festival, when the young men and women fetch a branch from the jungle, to the accompaniment of singing and dancing. It is erected in the village and decorated with lights and flowers. A feast is held, and when they have eaten and drunk, they spend the day in dancing and merriment round the branch. Next morning it is flung into the nearest stream, and with it the ill-luck of the village departs. The bamboo, on account of its many utilities, is also naturally an object of worship to the hillman. Darha, one of the chief gods of the Mundas and Oraons, is represented by a piece of split bamboo, stuck slantwise into the ground, which is regarded as the village watchman or patron. The influence of tree-worship among the jungle tribes may be estimated by the number of sept totems derived from this source found in the Bengal lists collected by Mr. Risley.

Tree-worship forms a large part of the animistic beliefs of the people of the plains, and many trees have been adopted into the worship of the higher gods, such as the Bel (*Aegle marmelos*), which is the sacred tree of Siva, and its leaves are so essential to the cult of the god and of his female consorts that no true follower of Vishnu will so much as mention its name. The pretty

Harrowing and Clod-crushing (p. 158)

little Tulsi plant, the holy basil, does the same service to Vishnu, and may be seen growing on a masonry pillar before the temples and homes of votaries of the god.

The many varieties of the fig genus, again, like the Banyan and the Pipal, are regarded as sacred by all Hindus, and are found growing near many shrines. In fact, the catalogue of holy trees is enormous, and there are few trees or plants of peculiar beauty, appearance, or interest, which are not in some way utilised for the purpose of ritual.

The awe and mystery of the jungle are impersonated in the many forest Mothers or goddesses who are revered by various tribes. One of the chief of these is Bansapti Ma, 'the Mistress of the Wood,' whose shrine is usually a pile of stones and branches of trees to which every passer-by contributes an offering. If he neglects to propitiate her in this way she sends one of her tigers to destroy him, and if any one dares to sing or whistle within her precincts she drives him mad. Hence she is venerated by herdsmen and woodcutters, who vow to sacrifice a cock, a goat, or a young pig, if she protects them and their cattle from beasts of prey. She is often identified with the dreaded Churel, the ghost of a woman dying in her confinement, or with the angry spirit of some one who has met his death in the jungle. Another form of these forest spirits is the Baghaut, the ghost of a man who has been killed by a tiger, while another dangerous creature haunts precipitous hill passes, and flings those who fail to do him honour into a ravine.

With the beginnings of settled life comes the worship of Mother Earth. She has two manifestations, being generally regarded as benignant, the mother of all things, the giver of food. But sometimes she brings disease and demands propitiation. She permits no evil spirit to rest upon her wide bosom, and hence the dying man is laid on the ground, and the mother at the time of her delivery, while newly wedded couples sleep on the ground for the first three months of married life. The herdsmen propitiate her by letting the first stream of milk fall on the ground, and as the building of a house disturbs her when the foundations are being dug, she must be worshipped when it is occupied for the first time, and also at the family rites of marriage and childbirth. In Bengal the chief festival in her honour is celebrated in the end of the hot season, when she is supposed to suffer from the impurity common to women. All ploughing, sowing, and other work cease during that time, and widows in Bengal refrain from eating cooked rice.

The chief periodical festivals of the Dravidians are celebrated with the object of stimulating her fertility. These are held at the critical times of the farming season—the sowing and transplanting of the rice, the harvest and the garnering of the produce, at which the youths and girls dance and pat the ground with their hands in order to rouse her to activity. One of these festivals, that of the Karam tree, has been already described. But more important is that in which the marriage of Mother Earth is solemnised. She has been provided with a male consort, known in many places as Bhūmiya, the Earth god. The Oraons wed her to the Sun in the early spring when the Sāl tree, held sacred by them, is in flower. The villagers, led by their tribal priest, visit the sacred grove, a remnant of the original forest in which they believe that the Old Woman of the Grove resides. She is supposed to have great influence over the rain, and is honoured with a sacrifice of five fowls. These altar presentations are cooked with rice, and a portion of the sacred food is distributed to all present. The girls collect the Sāl flowers and return laden with them to the hamlet. The priest next day makes a visit to each house, carrying the flowers in an open basket. The women of each household bring out water to wash his feet as he approaches, and kneeling before him make a most respectful obeisance. He then dances with them, and places some of the flowers over the house door and in the hair of the women. This done, they pour the contents of their water-vessels over him, and douse him heartily, the object being by a sort of sympathetic magic to promote the abundant fall of rain to refresh Mother Earth. Then, as at a regular marriage, the evening is spent in dancing and revelry. Celebrations of the same kind occur at the harvest season, when as a means of propitiating the goddess and promoting her fertility, wild orgies, in which for a time all rules of decency and self-respect are forgotten, prevail.

From the worship of this, the most primitive of the Mother goddesses, the cultus has been developed into that of the female energies of Nature, the foulest element in modern Hinduism. In secluded parts of the country, like the Central Provinces, we can watch the evolution of this form of worship. Here Devi, the goddess most usually worshipped in Northern India, is recognised to be identical with the Earth goddess, from whom the crops and the people derive their sustenance. She has as her consort Siva, whose phallic emblem clearly proves that the worship of this pair of deities is derived from the primitive conception by which the fertility of the soil is promoted.

But besides this benignant manifestation of the Mother goddess, she shows herself in her chthonic or malignant form. Among people who bury their dead it is easy to understand that the Earth goddess becomes connected with death and the ghost, and is regarded as the patron of disease, particularly that of an epidemic or unexpected nature. Hence she manifests herself as Mari Māta, 'Mother Death,' who presides over cholera, and as Sitala Māta, 'She that loves the cool,' in allusion to the fever which accompanies smallpox. The latter, in a land where vaccination is only beginning to be adopted, is the chiet scourge of infant life. Her little shrines may be seen in almost every hamlet, and at times when the plague is rife mothers hasten to propitiate her, or one of the seven sisters who are supposed to preside over various forms of the disease.

In this manifestation Devi develops into many shapes as she is pictured by an imaginative people. Most cruel and dangerous is Kāli, the dread goddess of death, before whom all Bengal crouches in terror.

All the inventiveness of a debased priesthood has been lavished in adding to the horror which she inspires. She is pictured as black in face, with a hideous expression, her lips dropping blood, her neck encircled with snakes, skulls, and heads of human victims. She represents Hindu polytheism in its most degraded shape. Dark stories are told of human victims offered to her in secluded shrines. And even now at her shrine in Calcutta and in the Thug temple at Bindhachal the blood of countless animals is never allowed to dry upon her altars.

While the worship of the Mother goddess in her divers forms is associated with the early stages of agricultural life, when the nomadic stage has passed and the people settle down in permanent villages, a new class of deities appears to which most of the homage of the peasantry is at present devoted. These are the Grāma-devata, or minor gods, 'godlings' as they have been called, of the village. The rural classes do indeed know the names and the attributes of some of the greater gods, like Vishnu and Siva. There may be in the more important villages a shrine to one or other of these, erected by some pious landholder or merchant and served by a Brahman priest. But worship here is confined to the higher classes, and the cultivator and labourer are content to propitiate the village deities.

These deities represent a very early conception, because they are a mob of spirits, many without any special name, and to few of them any distinct function has been assigned. It is at a much later stage that to each spirit a separate department is allotted. Again, the cult of these deities is quite distinct from that of the higher gods. No Brahman serves at their altars, the duty being left to the medicine-man. In times of trouble, when disease, drought, or famine prevails, even the higher classes will resort to the village shrine. But the offerings are usually made by women, who in India as elsewhere are the most conservative in matters of religion. A temple is seldom erected to deities of this kind. A pile of rough stones collected under a sacred tree is the usual altar. In Behar it is a mound or stone erected under a tree and smeared with vermilion. In the Bengal Delta the village spirit is represented by an earthen pot filled with water, with a mango twig placed on the top, and the whole covered with a piece of new cloth to keep out evil spirits. The usual offerings are a little milk and a share of the fruits of the earth, while at night a lamp is lighted at the shrine. It is only when serious danger menaces the village that a goat is slain. Its head is severed by a single blow, and with the blood dripping from it the head is laid upon the altar, while the flesh is cooked and consumed then and there in the presence of the god with whom his worshippers thus gain communion.

The characteristic of this form of worship is that it is purely local, each village having its own shrine and its own set of gods. Sometimes, of course, one of these acquires a wider vogue on account of cures performed at his shrine, or other mercies which have been vouchsafed by him. In this case the cultus is usually

A VILLAGE SCENE, BENGAL (p. 127)

taken over by a Brahman, and the village deity blossoms out into an incarnation or manifestation of one of the greater gods. But, as a rule, they are content to remain in obscurity, and this has the important effect of tying the Hindu down to his own village, whose gods he knows and can propitiate, and of making him averse to wander beyond it into the domain of strange powers whose worship he does not understand. Those village gods in Bengal who have secured a wider range than the confines of the village are those which are believed to inhabit trees, to which pieces of rag are tied as an offering to secure the welfare of children.

But besides this group of deities all representing the manifestations of Nature, Animism has created a class of spirits of quite another type. These are, first, the vague spiritual beings which inhabit the air, sometimes visit earth, and are inimical to the human race; secondly, the ghosts of the dead, some of whom are kindly, others malignant.

The former class seems to represent the vague horror which seizes people in the depths of the jungle or in the desert wilds. An example of these is the Rākshasa, who in some respects corresponds to the Jinn of Arabian folk-lore, who themselves have been imported with the Mohammedan invaders. A passage in the epic of the *Mahabharata* describes them as 'fierce, tawny in hue, terrible, with adamantine teeth, and dyed with blood. Their locks were matted on their heads, their thighs were long and massive; they had five feet, and their bellies were large. Their fingers were turned backwards, their temper harsh, their features ugly, their voice loud and terrible. They had rows of tinkling bells tied to their waists; their throats were blue and terrible.' In the paintings of the Ajanta caves, executed in the later Buddhist period, the female, or Rākshasi, is represented as a goblin in the shape of a handsome woman, red, fair, or dark, with flowing hair, killing men and feeding on their flesh and blood. In the folk-tales they are always represented as cannibals; but like such monsters all the world over, they are silly and can be easily deceived. Even nowadays the spirits of men of evil life are believed to become Rākshasas; but, as a rule, they are distinct from the ordinary malignant ghost.

The Deo is, like the Rākshasa, a cannibal. He is known by his long lips, one of which sticks up in the air, while the other hangs pendent. He often causes tempests, and were he not stupid by nature, could work infinite mischief. Such demons often occupy trees, and bound down upon luckless passers-by at night, or with their hooked claws drag them up into the branches. The Daitya is another tree-haunter. In front he looks like a man, but seen from behind he is hollow, a mere husk without a backbone. At midnight he is often seen flying from one tree to another in a flash of fire and smoke.

The ordinary ghost is a being of quite another type. When the soul leaves the body it is believed to haunt for a time the place of death. It wanders about in a state of miserable restlessness, an unhappy little creature no larger than a man's thumb, awaiting the preparation of its new body by the rite of the Srāddha. In this stage it is, unless duly propitiated, inclined to be malignant; but it usually ends by being included among the Pitri, or sainted dead, who are kindly and protective.

During the intermediate stage of the soul many of the jungle and menial tribes spread ashes on the floor of the hut. On this is placed a lamp hidden under a basket. The son of the dead man goes outside the hut at night, and turning in the direction by which the corpse was removed, calls the name of the dead loudly two or three times. This is the only occasion on which they dare to name the dead, because it may lead to unpleasant visits from them. Often the spirit answers out of the darkness, and its presence in the house is indicated by little footsteps on the ashes. His appearance is a sign that he died a natural death, and not through evil magic or by the attacks of a Bhūt. Food is presented to him, and he is invited to eat and bless his posterity.

It is different with those who die after an evil life, by some accident, or those who have been deprived of funeral rites. Such is the Pisācha, an evil spirit the result of man's vices, the ghost of a liar, an adulterer, or criminal, or of one who has died insane. The Bhūt, again, is the spirit of one who has died by violence, by suicide, or has suffered execution. The malignancy of such a spirit is increased if the body has not been buried or cremated according to the laws of the caste or tribe. Not that all who die by violence become Bhūts. The warrior slain on the field of battle goes straight to the home of the ancestral spirits; but he who dies of love haunts a banyan-tree. Another ghost of this class is the Gayāl, he who dies without a son to perform his funeral rites, and is hence naturally spiteful and obnoxious to the sons of other people. Mothers soothe his wrath by pouring little offerings of milk and Ganges water into depressions on his altar.

The Bhūt is generally testy and ill-humoured because he has been swept from the world before his due time. He resents the second marriage of his widow, which must be performed at night, and she wears an amulet as a protective. In popular belief he is a foul creature who eats carrion, and as he is always thirsty he drinks water no matter how impure it may be. He casts no shadow, speaks with a nasal tone, and can be most readily scared by the savour of burning turmeric. Writing of Bengal, Mr. Gait remarks that when a Bhūt has been brought under control by an exorcist, 'he is a valuable possession and a marketable commodity—the usual price being about Rs. 20.' When the sale of a Bhūt has been arranged, the Ojha exorcist hands over a corked bamboo cyclinder which is supposed to contain him. This is taken to a place, usually a tree, where it is intended he should in future reside; a small ceremony is performed, liquor being poured on the ground, or small mounds erected in his honour, and the cork is then taken out, whereupon the Bhūt is supposed to take up his abode in the place chosen

No. 29

Women Husking Rice, Chota Nagpur (p. 169)

for him. His function is to watch the crops and guard them from thieves, and if any one should be hardy enough to steal from a tree thus guarded, he is certain to be stricken by the Bhūt, and in a few days will sicken or die.'

The most dangerous of male Bhūts is the Barham, or Brahma Rākshasa, the ghost of a Brahman who has died a violent death. 'Such spirits,' Mr. Gait goes on to say, 'are specially powerful and malicious. Sometimes they are represented as a headless trunk, with the eyes looking from the breast. They are believed to inhabit large trees by the side of a river or in some lonely place, where they throw stones at travellers and lead them astray on dark nights, and woe betide the unfortunate who should give them cause for offence, as by unwittingly felling the tree in which he has taken up his abode, or who was in any way responsible for his death. He can only escape the evil consequences by making the Barham his family god and worshipping him regularly. In Behar he often becomes the tutelary deity of the whole village. The worship is usually performed under a tree, usually a banyan, which he is supposed to frequent. The trunk is painted vermilion, and a mound of earth is erected, on which are placed clay figures of horses or elephants, and offerings are made of flowers, betel-nuts, and the like. The worship is conducted by a special priest, who is not necessarily a Brahman, and occasionally he is inspired by the spirit and utters prophecies, which are implicitly believed in by the devotees.' Some of these Brahman ghosts who are specially malignant, being the spirits of men who have perished as the result of persecution or in some peculiarly tragical way, attain a repute beyond the narrow circle of their original worshippers, and the cult of some of these, who have reached the dignity of national gods, is still spreading widely.

From the world of spirits which hold such a high place in Hindu belief, we pass to the animal creation. As has been already said, people in this stage of culture draw no clear line between the human and the animal. In their belief animals manifest an intelligence which is much higher than our conception of instinct. Special animals thus come to be worshipped, some because of their utility to man, others on account of the awe and wonder which they inspire. The most obvious example of the first class is the cow, and although the taboo which protects her is of comparatively modern origin, it is no less effective on that account. In the second class stand animals like the tiger and the snake, the worship of which is based simply on terror. When the tiger is a man-eater, he is often believed to be some dangerous sorcerer metamorphosed. His worship is naturally common among the jungle tribes who are exposed to his attacks. They fear to mention his name or replace it by some euphemistic epithet. Some of them will not join the sportsmen in hunting the beast, and when one is killed they solemnly address him, and pray to him that, being now a spirit, he will continue to spare their cattle and themselves.

The Gonds have a tiger god, Bāgh Deo, and a special class of medicine-man or priest is believed to be able to control the animal and protect his parishioners from attack.

Although in this part of India the cult has been less highly developed than in the south, serpent-worship is an important part of the popular beliefs. The snake is conceived in two ways. From his habit of gliding in and out of the hut, and from the mysterious wisdom which he is supposed to possess, he comes to be regarded as one of the forms in which the ancestors of the household appear. Hence he guards the house, and in particular the family treasure. Secondly, he is fearsome and uncanny, an idea to which his tortuous motion, the cold fixity of his gaze, the suddenness and deadliness of his attack contribute. He is particularly dreaded by women who encounter him in the fields and in the dark corners of their huts.

Feelings such as these have led to the creation of special gods, who control snakes. The greatest of these is in Bengal, Manasa, who, says Mr. Gait, 'is benignant, if properly propitiated, but if neglected, or the ceremony in her honour is not performed with strict observance of rule, it is said that some one of the family is certain to die of snake-bite. She is worshipped in various forms. Sometimes a simple earthen pot is marked with vermilion and placed under a tree, where clay snakes are arranged round it and a trident is driven into the ground; sometimes the plant called after her is taken as her emblem, and sometimes an image of a small four-armed figure of yellow colour, her feet resting on a goose, a cobra in each hand, and a tiara of snakes on her head. Sometimes she is believed to take up her abode in a pipal-tree. In places where snakes abound, most families have a shrine dedicated to her in their homes, and sometimes a separate room is set apart for her.' Among the higher castes the worship is performed by a Brahman; but the menial castes conduct the service themselves, and the priest is often inspired by the goddess and utters oracles. It is a common practice to draw a holy circle with cow-dung to represent a snake round the house, which is henceforth safe from attack.

It is difficult to say where animal-worship of this kind ends and totemism begins, and it is very doubtful whether totemism does form an important element in the popular religion.

This hasty sketch of Animism will explain the character of the belief. It forms the basis of the standard religions, largely represented in modern Hinduism, and to a less degree in Mohammedanism, save among converts drawn from the lower strata of the people. The processes by which these Animistic beliefs come to be overlain by, and gradually absorbed into, the standard religions has been already indicated. In Bengal, where, more than in any other part of Northern India, Animism persists in its crudest form among the compact, well-organised forest tribes, the stages of the evolution can be most clearly traced. The religion of a tribe mainly depends upon its environment. Secluded in a wild country like Chota

Nagpur, it is little affected by Hinduism; in the plains it gradually succumbs to the foreign influences which surround it.

This is shown by the nature of the tribal priesthood. Among some tribes, like the Korwas, the head of the household performs the service of the local gods, and the only priest is a medicine-man whose functions are defined merely in the vaguest way. Then comes the stage when a regular official, half priest, half exorcist, is employed. This office is often hereditary, and thus the way is open for the occasional employment of a Brahman when the tribe adopts the external observances of Hinduism, while the service of the minor gods continues to be performed by a tribesman.

Later comes the stage at which all religious duties are monopolised by the Brahman. Under his influence the cultus develops with all that luxuriance which shows itself in Oriental faiths, and it ends in the establishment of a crowd of deities, the functions and attributes of one merging in or being identified with those of another, until the student is almost tempted to abandon in despair any hope of arranging them on a consistent plan. To people of the West who have reduced theology to a science, and regulate it by definite creeds, such a system of belief appears intolerable. But the Hindu looks on the matter from quite a different point of view. The vagueness of the conception is to him its greatest merit, and there are no indications that his view is likely to be seriously modified in the immediate future.

CHAPTER XIV

MAGIC, SHAMANISM, WITCHCRAFT

Magic: its origin: its relation to Religion. Magic, White and Black. Imitative Magic. Magic by images. Rain-making. Nudity. Hair loosed. Contagious Magic. Identification of the magician. Magical spells. Black Magic. Controlling a demon. The charmed circle. Shamanism. Devil-dancing. Exorcism of disease. The village witch.

It is difficult to realise the extent to which the people of Northern India are in bondage to the various modes of belief grouped together under the head of Magic. As Mr. E. S. Hartland has recently shown, it depends on the qualities which the savage believes to be associated with every personality. There is no exact Indian term for what the Melanesians call Mana, the potentiality and atmosphere which everything, human and material, is supposed to possess. The successful warrior or hunter, and even less important and successful men, all possess it. 'Every one,' Mr. Hartland writes, 'is conscious of powers of some sort, and every one would attribute to others capabilities larger or smaller. Some would possess in their own consciousness and in the eyes of their fellows a very small modicum of power for good or evil. The mere glance or voice of others would inspire terror or confidence. This potentiality, this atmosphere, would often cling with greater in-

Bathing in the Ganges, Hardwar (p. 227)

tensity to non-human beings, objective or imaginary. The snake, the bird, the elephant, the sun, the invisible wind, the unknown wielder of the lightning, would be richly endowed. None, human or non-human, would, in theory at least, be wholly without it.'

These considerations bring us to the explanation of beliefs such as Magic, Shamanism, Witchcraft, the Evil Eye, and Omens. Certain people, certain things are believed not only to possess this mysterious influence, but to be able to project their potentiality so as to affect the lives of others. It is obvious that such beliefs are very closely allied to Animism. Magic and religion among savage and semi-savage races spring from the same root and develop on parallel lines. Among the forest tribes, for instance, it is impossible to draw the line between Magic and Religion, and the practitioner, Baiga, Pahan, or Ojha, is at once priest and medicine-man.

At a later period, of course, these two streams of belief, originating from a common source, tend to flow apart. As soon as the conception of a vague mob of spirits gives way to a system of departmental gods, the magician who works without the aid of the gods becomes distinguished from the priest who claims to have discovered the methods of placating or coercing them. But even in the higher grades of Hinduism this stage has not been reached. The Brahman, for instance, relies more upon the Mantra, or spell, than upon the prayer. These Mantras form the great apparatus which is used in the most degraded form of Hindu belief, that known as the Tantrik, which is concerned with the worship of the female energies of Nature,

In India, as in other parts of the world, a clear distinction is drawn between what are commonly known as White and Black Magic. The former is a recognised method of promoting the interests of the community, as, for instance, in rain-making and by other devices for the general benefit of all members of the tribe. It is different when any one who has gained this power employs it for his own interest—to bring others under his power, to punish an enemy or a rival. This is Black Magic, or Witchcraft, which is naturally regarded as an offence against the community at large. The worker of such arts is regarded as a common danger, a public enemy, and is ruthlessly persecuted.

Magic in both these forms depends on two principles; one, that like produces like, or that an effect resembles its cause, producing Homœopathic or Imitative Magic; secondly, that things which have once been in contact continue to act on each other even after the contact has been severed, producing Contagious Magic. Both these varieties are fully developed in Northern India.

As an example of Imitative Magic we may take the method by which the magician seeks to injure his enemy by operating upon a figure of him, in the belief that as it wastes he dies, as it perishes he perishes. The Tantrik magician makes the figure in wax, and inscribes on every joint of it the meaningless but mystic word 'Hri.' He writes the name of his enemy upon the breast and there fixes the bone of a dead man. The whole he buries in a cremation ground, and covers it with the ashes of the dead. The result will be that the Mana proceeding from the corpse will be communicated to his enemy, who becomes mad, leaves his home in a frenzy, sickens and pines away, and can be restored to health only when the image is removed from its deadly surroundings.

The methods of the Mohammedan are similar. He takes earth from a grave or from a Hindu cremation place; makes a doll a span long and repeats the 105th chapter of the Korān, or the 111th said backwards over twenty-one wooden skewers, which he drives into various parts of the image. This is shrouded in the manner of a corpse, and buried in the name of the enemy, who, it is believed, will surely die.

Even jungle tribes, like the Bhīls, employ similar means. When they have continuous bad luck in hunting they make an image of a man, or sometimes of a man and a woman, in the sand or dust of a jungle path. Over this they pile straw or grass, set it on fire, and with much abuse and uproar beat the images with sticks. This they call 'Killing Bad Luck.'

One important branch of Imitative Magic is rain-making, and this illustrates two conditions of successful Magic; one, that the body of the performer should be nude; the other, that the hair should be loose and flowing. The magician being exposed to taboo, the rule of enforced nudity in magical rites is probably based on the theory that the clothes are likely to convey the Mana of others, a condition which we inadequately express by the terms 'pollution' or 'impurity.' In the most interesting form of the rain-making rite in Northern India, women go at night with a plough into the fields, strip off all their garments, and drag the plough some distance through the soil, with invocations to the rain-god to remove the drought and permit the regular ploughing to proceed. The natives regard the removal of the clothing as an extreme act of submission to the deity whom they address. But the analogy of similar instances of ritual nudity in India seems to show that 'pollution' is at the root of the matter. This probably explains why Fakīrs, before the habit was repressed by British law, used to go about in a state of nudity.

The women, also, while performing this magical rite, let their hair flow loose over their shoulders. The sanctity of witches, wizards, and the like is supposed to rest in the hair. Hence the careful rules for cutting it after childbirth and on visits to places of pilgrimage. Magic can be worked through hair, and at the bathing fairs an important part of the ritual is the ceremonial shaving of the bathers. Those who are specially careful consign their locks to the stream which is believed to protect from evil influence. Others leave it where it falls, supposing that the holy atmosphere which surrounds the holy place will remove the possibility of danger. We see this belief in the 'sanctity' of the hair in the case of many Fakīrs who never shave or cut it, and keep it in unkempt masses flowing over their shoulders. An appeal is often made to magistrates to prevent an enemy from 'growing his hair' to the injury of the plaintiff. The terror which people exhibit when this mode of coercion is practised against them proves that it is believed to be effective.

Other methods of rain-making illustrate the principles of Imitative Magic. We have seen that the Oraon priest at the Sarhūl festival, as he visits each house in the village, is doused with water by the women, the intention obviously being to secure an abundant fall of rain. In the Punjab the village girls pour down on an old woman water mixed with the dung of the sacred cow. It is part of the charm that the victim should abuse her persecutors. Or a crone is made to sit under the house eaves and get drenched when the first shower falls. In a more advanced stage of belief the same result is produced by sinking a Brahman up to his lips in a tank and making him invoke the rain-god until he answers by a downpour. Or a Fakīr is seated in a trench and kept there until, as the people say, the god relents on seeing the sufferings of the holy man and grants him relief. Another plan is to hang a frog, the animal which by its croaking announces and therefore is supposed to bring the rain, from a bamboo, or to douse the Lingam image of Siva and pour water on the grave of a bachelor Brahman. In a famous temple in Western India the enclosure contains a Fire Pit, a Rain Pit, and a Wind Pit, in which the spirits which cause these phenomena are supposed to be contained. When heat fails the Fire Pit is opened, and the same course is taken to secure wind and rain.

The varieties of this Imitative Magic are innumerable. All the domestic rites, birth, marriage, death are full of practices of this kind. The pair are married to trees, the wedding of the Earth goddess is celebrated, the new well is wedded to the trees which it is to water—all devices based upon the same train of thought.

Passing from Imitative to Contagious Magic, a good example of the latter is to be found in the theory that a man may be injured by placing something upon his footmarks, which are supposed to be an integral part of his personality. The forest tribes of the central hills have many devices of this kind, and allege that they know the special things which, so placed, will cause various kinds of disease. They look suspiciously on any one who examines the marks after they have passed along a jungle path. In the plains this method is employed to remove epidemic disease from a sick child. The cross-roads are the place where the charm works best. A few scales from the body of a person attacked by smallpox are placed on a little pile of earth in the middle of the road and decorated with flowers. Any one who touches such things is believed to take the malady with him, and so relieve the patient.

Magic of this kind is used most commonly in the case of disease. The popular theory is that it is due to an evil spirit, or to the machinations of some wizard. When a person sickens, the first stage of the cure is to ascertain who is responsible for his illness. To discover this, various devices are employed. In Chota Nagpur, when an Ojha, or exorcist, is summoned for

Pilgrims Conveying Ganges Water (p. 227)

this purpose, he either calls in the aid of a brother in the craft, or brings with him one or two disciples who have a smattering of the art. A bell-metal tray is produced and filled with pure water, into which a small handful of coarse pulse is thrown. The dish is placed in the sun, and the Ojha, repeating incantations in a whisper, so that the sacred words may not reach any one who is ill disposed, stares steadily into the dish, observing the shadow cast by the grains floating on the surface. After some time he retires to a short distance, and his place is taken by one of his assistants, who does the like. The Ojha then proceeds to question him as to what he sees. There is, of course, collusion between the parties, and by and by the person whom it was arranged to denounce, generally a widow or childless woman, is named. It is useless for her to protest. In former days she would certainly have been murdered. At present she escapes with a beating, and is forced to agree to remove the spell.

Among the Santāls the method was to take branches of the Sāl, the sacred tree of the tribe, and to mark them with the names of all the females in the village, whether married or unmarried, who had attained the age of twelve years, and to fix them in water, where they remained for four and a half hours. The withering of any branch was a proof of witchcraft against the woman whose name it bore. Another plan was to tie up small portions of rice in pieces of cloth marked as before, and to place them in a white ant's nest. The consumption of the grain in any packet was a sign of guilt. Sometimes, again, lamps were lighted at night;

water was poured into leaf-cups, and mustard oil let fall drop by drop upon the water, while the name of each woman in the village was pronounced. If the Ojha identified her shadow in the water, the woman was held guilty.

When a Bhīl dies, the Bhopa, or witch-finder, is called in, seated on a wooden platform, and near him is placed a large earthen pot with a brass dish covering the mouth. This is beaten by two men of the tribe, who at the same time sing the funeral dirge. The spirit of the deceased is now supposed to enter the Bhopa, and through him to demand what it wants. If the man has died by a natural death, his spirit calls for milk, and repeats through the Bhopa the words he used just before death. But if he has died through violence or evil magic, he calls for his bow, arrows, and gun to revenge his own death. Then the Bhopa works himself up into a frenzy, going through the motions of firing the gun and shouting the war-cry, by which he indicates to the survivors the person who is responsible, and causes to him the pain which his victim has experienced.

Great reliance is placed upon the spoken word or spell, which carries with it the potentiality of the person who invented it or uses it, or of the deity whose name appears in it. A few examples may be given of spells used to remove disease, charm animals, and for other purposes. To cure headache the patient is ordered to repeat the following invocation a certain number of times: 'I bind the river, its bank, the vegetation which grows upon it! I bind the earth a cubit and a quarter deep! O divine preceptor! aid me!' For toothache:—'Teeth, teeth! You are thirty-two! What quarrel is between us? I will do the earning, you may do the eating, and live happily with me till I die.' Fever, the bane of the peasant, is naturally regarded as the act of a spirit, which must be scared before the patient can recover. One prescription directs him to take a fly, bruise it up with black pepper, asafœtida, and water, and to apply the mixture to the eye. The smell and pungency will affright the spirit, which will depart with the fly. A device to cure blindness, based on the same train of thought, prescribes that the patient should take the feather of an owl and some incense, burn it in a packet made of black cloth soaked in butter. The ashes are to be applied to the eye of the patient. Another remedy for fever is to pluck on a Sunday the berry of the Stramonium or Dhatūra, which has narcotic and soothing effects, and tie it on the right wrist of the sick man. Scavengers, when they suffer from rheumatism, kill a kite on a Tuesday, and tie the bones with a string round the aching limb. The pain flies away with the spirit of the bird. Lastly, if you can count all the leaves on a Nīm tree (*Azidirachta indica*), it is said that you will get rid of fever, which is not improbable. The snake has great virtue in charms like these. There is one variety which is popularly supposed to have a head at both ends. Wet a cloth in its blood, dry it in the sun, make a ball of it, put it into your mouth, and you will be able to walk on water.

Some Bhopas and Baigas among the forest tribes, in order to keep up their reputation, pretend to possess spells which give them mastery over the tiger and other beasts of prey. One approved charm runs as follows: 'Bind the tiger, bind the tigress, bind her seven cubs! Bind the road, the footpath, the fields through which they wander! Aid us, O Lord Krishna, and Lona Chamārin! (a noted witch).' Bathe seven times on seven Tuesdays. If you then meet a tiger it will not harm you, and by virtue of this spell you may even enter his den. But the result is very doubtful.

Devices of this kind are of the nature of White Magic, and are approved by the people. Is is different with Black Magic, which is applied to some selfish or evil purpose.

The intention of many of these rites is to bring a demon or evil spirit into subservience to the will of the performer. We may take an instance from Bengal. It will be noticed that the corpse and the burial-ground enter largely into rites of this kind. When a man dies on the fifteenth day of the month, being Saturday, an ill-omened day controlled by the god Sani or Saturn, the performer with his teacher should go to the cremation ground. The teacher sits on a tree at a short distance, while the performer approaches the corpse, and lays it on the ground with its feet turned to the south, the land of spirits. He should then tie down the hands and feet of the corpse with iron pegs driven deep into the ground. He sits on its breast with a bottle of spirits beside him, and

No. 32

Sacrificing a Goat to the Goddess Devi, Chota Nagpur (p. 134)

recites Mantras, or spells, on a rosary made of pieces of bone. When these have been repeated one hundred and eight times, he drinks some of the spirits and pours a little into the mouth of the corpse, whereupon it will make faces at him and try to get up and attack him. He must all this time keep calling out to his teacher and follow the instructions which he gives, remembering that if he only keeps up his courage he can suffer no harm. He should go on reciting the spells and drinking the liquor, and at the close of each period of one hundred and eight recitals animals of hideous shape will appear. He is to pay no heed to them, until at last a cat comes and asks him what he needs. To this he answers that he requires the services of the spirit of the corpse on which he is seated. This boon the cat grants him. He is then to make a fire sacrifice, at which he offers flesh and liquor, and rubs his forehead with the ashes of the sacrificial fire. He may then return home, assured that the spirit will do his bidding for the rest of his life. But he must be careful not to look back, lest the vagrant ghosts which haunt the place may seize him. Such are the nightmare-like orgies of the Tantrik magician, the effect of which doubtless depends upon the amount of liquor which the performer imbibes.

Mohammedans follow practices of much the same kind. In Gujarat it is held essential that the worker of Black Magic should never cleanse his body, lest he may lose his power; he must never bathe, use perfumes, pray, or approve of any action which is good or virtuous. At the Diwāli, or Feast of Lamps, in September-October, evil spirits are free to revisit their haunts on earth, especially on the fourteenth day of the dark fortnight in the month of Kārttik. On that night the warlock puts on the dirtiest apparel, anoints himself with evil-smelling oils, and providing himself with a knife and hamper of vile food—beef, mutton, and entrails—with large quantities of incense, starts for the haunt of evil spirits, which is the graveyard of low-caste people or the burial-place of executed murderers. On reaching the place he makes a charmed circle, within which he sits with his knife ready. He begins to recite his spells, and flings grains of black pulse round him. By and by the spirits assemble, and he asks them which kind of food they prefer. If they select any of the kinds he has at hand, he flings morsels to them from the circle within which he sits. Occasionally they demand human flesh, in which case he must cut a piece from his own thigh and throw it to them. If he fail to do this, he runs the risk of being torn to pieces by them. If any spirit accepts the flesh of the warlock, he becomes his slave for a year. 'Sometimes,' writes the native authority on whose statement this account is based, 'a sorcerer unwilling to cut off his own flesh, persuades a pupil or a friend to go with him. If the spirit requires human flesh, the sorcerer offers his companion as a victim, on condition the spirit spares the victim till he reaches his home. The spirit agrees, and when the séance is over follows his victim, and at the victim's house kills him by eating his liver. Next morning the victim is found dead, having thrown up broken pieces of his eaten liver like clots of blood.'

In all the modes of Black Magic the charmed circle within which the warlock sits is the protective on which he most relies. Among the jungle tribes and menial castes in the plains such a circle is very commonly drawn round a house or village to ward off cholera and other epidemic disease. This line, formed of milk and spirits, the demon which brings the disease cannot cross. The same precaution is adopted annually in the jungle villages to bar the roads against the entrance of spirits belonging to another settlement, which, being strangers, are presumably hostile. It is even drawn round a refractory debtor who cannot, it is supposed, cross the mystic barrier until he has satisfied the demands of his creditor.

The rites of Black Magic often follow those of Imitative Magic. Thus when Mohammedan women desire to destroy an enemy, they go to a mosque on a Friday and place there a brick upside down, with an invocation that their enemy's house may be overturned as the brick is. Or they put some lime on the wall of the mosque, praying that it may get into the enemy's eye and blind him.

The Shaman, medicine-man, wizard, or warlock, is recognised as the agent who controls the unseen spiritual powers and compels them to cure disease, foretell the future, rule the weather, avenge a man upon his enemy, and generally intervene for good or evil in human affairs. 'The conception of the character of the power invoked,' says Mr. Risley, 'varies with the culture of the people themselves. They may be gods or demons, spirits or ancestral ghosts, or their nature may be wholly obscure and shadowy. In order to place himself *en rapport* with them, the Shaman lives a life apart, practises or pretends to practise various austerities, wears mysterious and symbolical garments, and performs noisy incantations in which a sacred drum or an enchanted rattle takes a leading part. On occasion he should be able to foam at the mouth and go into a trance or fit, during which his soul is supposed to quit his body and wander away into space.' By some these seizures have been ascribed to epilepsy, but some of the phenomena seem to be hypnotic.

The methods of exorcising evil spirits are found most fully developed in Southern India, where they have been described by Bishop Caldwell and Dr. A. C. Burnell under the name of Devil-dancing. In a less elaborate form they are the stock-in-trade of the Northern Indian exorcist. Thus among the Kurs of Bengal the Baiga collects the people to aid him in the invocation. Dancing and music are followed by a seizure, which passes like a contagion among the spectators. Among the Mundas all disease in men and cattle is attributed to one of two causes: the wrath of some evil spirit which must be appeased, or the spell of some witch or sorcerer who must be destroyed or driven out of the land. In the latter case the Sokha, or witch-finder, is employed to divine who has cast the spell. He employs various methods, one of the most common being the test by the stone and wooden vessel ordinarily used to measure grain. This last is placed as a pivot on which the stone which it supports may revolve. A boy is seated on the stone, supporting himself by his hands, and the names of all suspected people in the neighbourhood are slowly pronounced. As each name is mentioned a few grains of rice are thrown at the boy. Suddenly he falls into a state of hypnotic coma and rolls off the stone. The person whose name is called just at that moment is denounced.

Many similar methods are used in diagnosing cases of disease characterised by the suddenness of the attack and the fits, paroxysms, or insensibility with which they are accompanied. The Indo-Tibetan tribes of North Assam cause the exorcist to lay out thirteen leaves, each with a few grains of corn upon it, and each identified with one particular spirit. Squatting before the leaves, he causes a pendulum attached to his thumb to vibrate before them, repeating invocations all the time. The spirit which has caused the disease is identified when the pendulum halts at any particular leaf. This is taken aside, and the exorcist inquires from the spirit what sacrifice he requires. It answers through its earthly representative, and the animal is made over to him by the friends of the patient. But with the canniness of this race the sacrifice is not performed until the patient recovers. The Nāgas are less cautious. When their exorcist is called in, he feels the patient's pulse, looks sapient, and decides which spirit must be appeased and how it is to be done. If a fowl be accepted as the sacrifice, the wizard kills, roasts, and eats it at once on the spot where the sick man was first taken ill. He throws what he cannot eat to the vagrant spirits hovering in the jungle close by. If the animal selected be a pig or dog, and he cannot then and there consume it all himself, he invites some friends to assist him, and if it be a buffalo, he gives a grand dinner-party.

Lastly, we come to the Dain, or village witch, who has no pretensions to knowledge of the mystic craft which the regular warlock claims. She is found in almost every village in the hill-country and in the plains, and though the people are shy about talking of her, her influence is generally recognised, especially by anxious mothers, who attribute to her machinations or to the Evil Eye which she casts the mysterious convulsions and similar maladies to which infant life is exposed. She is merely some eccentric, lonely, half-crazy, or malformed crone who is supposed to envy the prosperity of her neighbours, and chiefly the possession of a male heir. It is believed that she can blast the crops, bring disease on men and cattle, introduce something from outside or extract something out of the human body; that she can destroy the efficacy of religious rites. Amulets, disguises of the name and sex of children, are commonly used to thwart her maliciousness. In former days she would have been branded, blood drawn from her breast, her hair clipped; she would have been ducked in the village pond, or forced to undergo many cruel ordeals and persecutions. But British law, though it often fails to remedy many of the wrongs of village life, has at any rate succeeded in saving the reputed witch from evils greater than those of boycotting and the suspicion and ill-will which are the fate of this wretch and her sisters in many parts of the world.

BIBLIOGRAPHY

ATKINSON, E. T., *Himalayan Gazetteer*, 3 vols., 1882-84.

BADEN-POWELL, B. H., *The Indian Village Community*, 1896.

BALL, V., *Jungle Life in India*, 1880.

BANNERMAN, Captain A. D., *Report on Census of Rajputana*, 1902.

BIDDULPH, Major J., *Tribes of the Hindoo Koosh*, 1880.

BILLINGTON, Miss M. F., *Woman in India*, 1895.

BRADLEY-BIRT, F. B., *Chota Nagpore, a little-known Province of the Empire*, 1903.

—— *The Story of an Indian Upland*, 1905.

BUCHANAN, F., *Eastern India*, ed. M. MARTIN, 3 vols., 1838.

—— *Account of the Kingdom of Nepal*, 1819.

BURN, R., *Report on Census of North-western Provinces and Oudh* (*The United Provinces of Agra and Oudh*), 1902.

CAMPBELL, Major-Gen. J., *A Personal Narrative of Thirteen Years' Service among the Wild Tribes of Khondistan*, 1865.

COOPER, T. T., *The Mishmee Hills*, 1873.

CROOKE, W., *Tribes and Castes of the North-western Provinces and Oudh*, 4 vols., 1896.

DALAL, J. A., *Report on Census of Baroda*, 1902.

DALTON, Col. E. T., *Descriptive Ethnology of Bengal*, 1872.

DREW, F., *The Jummoo and Kashmir Territories*, 1875.

ENTHOVEN, R. E., *Report on Census of Bombay*, 1902.

FORBES, J., *Oriental Memoirs, a Narrative of Seventeen Years' Residence in India*, second edition, 1834.

FORSYTH, Captain J., *The Highlands of Central India*, second edition, 1889.

GAIT, E. A., *Report on Census of Assam*, 1892.

—— „ „ *Bengal*, 1902.

Gazetteer of Bombay, ed. Sir J. CAMPBELL, v.d.

„ *Central Provinces*, ed. C. Grant, 1870.

„ *Rajputana*, 3 vols., v.d.

GERARD, Captain A., *Account of Koonawur in the Himalaya*, 1841.

GODDEN, Miss G. M., *Naga and other Frontier Tribes of North-east India, Journal Anthropological Institute*, xxvi.-xxvii.

GORE, F. ST. G., *Lights and Shadows of Hill-life in the Afghan and Hindu Highlands of the Punjab*, 1895.

GRIERSON, G., *Bihar Peasant Life*, 1885.

GROWSE, F. S., *Mathura, a District Memoir*, third edition, 1883.

GUNTHORPE, Major E. J., *Notes on the Criminal Tribes of Bombay, Berar, and the Central Provinces*, 1882.

HARCOURT, Captain A. P. F., *The Himalayan Districts of Kooloo, Lahoul, and Spiti*, 1871.

HISLOP, Rev. S., *Papers regarding the Aboriginal Tribes of the Central Provinces*, 1866.

HOLDICH, Sir T. H., *The Indian Borderland*, 1901.

HOOKER, Sir J. D., *Himalayan Journals*, 2 vols., 1858.

HUGHES-BULLER, R., *Report on the Census of Baluchistan*, 1902.

HUNTER, Sir W. W., *Annals of Rural Bengal*, 1868.

—— *Orissa*, 2 vols., 1872.

IBBETSON, Sir D. C. J., *Punjab Ethnography*, 1883.

KNOWLES, Rev. S., *The Gospel in Gonda*, 1889.

LEWIN, Captain T. H., *Hill Tracts of Chittagong*, 1869.

—— *Wild Tribes of South-east India*, 1870.

LLOYD, Sir W. and GERARD A., *Journey from Caunpoor to the Boorendo Pass*, 2 vols., 1840.

LUARD, Captain C. E., *Report on the Census of Central India*, 1902.

LYALL, Sir A., *Asiatic Studies*, 2 vols., 1899.

MACLAGAN, E. D., *Report on the Census of the Punjab*, 1892.

MACPHERSON, Major S. C., *Memorials of Service in India*, 1865.

MALCOLM, Sir J., *Memoir of Central India*, 2 vols. 1823.

North Indian Notes and Queries, 5 vols., 1891-96.

OLDFIELD, H. A., *Sketches from Nipal*, 2 vols., 1880.

OLIVER, E. E., *Across the Border; or, Pathan and Biloch*, 1890.

Punjab Notes and Queries, 4 vols., 1883-87.

RISLEY, H. H., *Tribes and Castes of Bengal*, 2 vols., 1891.

—— *Report on the Census of India*, 1903.

ROBERTSON, Sir G., *The Kafirs of the Hindu Kush*, 1896.

ROSE, H. A., *Report on the Census of the Punjab*, 1902.

RUSSEL, R. V., *Report on the Census of the Central Provinces*, 1902.

SHERRING, C. A., *Western Tibet and the British Borderland*, 1906.

SLEEMAN, Col. W. H., *Rambles and Recollections of an Indian Official*, ed. V. A. SMITH, 2 vols., 1893.

SORABJI, Miss C., *Sun Babies, Studies in Indian Child Life*, 1904.

THORBURN, S. S., *Bannu; or, Our Afghan Frontier*, 1876.

[THORNTON, E.], *Illustrations of the History and Practices of th Thugs*, 1837.

WADDELL, Major L. A., *Among the Himalayas*, 1899.

—— *The Buddhism of Tibet, or Lamaism*, 1895.

WILSON, A., *The Abode of Snow*, 1875.

WISE, J., *Notes on the Races, Castes, and Trades of Eastern Bengal*, 1883.

INDEX

ABOR tribe, 37.
Afghan tribe, 58.
Agaria tribe, 133.
Agriculture, 129.
Aheri tribe, 142.
Ahīr caste, 115.
Aka tribe, 37.
Amusements, 187 ff.
Ancestral spirits, feeding of, 213.
Angāmi Nāga tribe, 38.
Animal life, respect for, 181.
Animism, 224 f.
—— adopted into the higher religions, 244.
Anthropometry, 18 f.
Ao tribe, 40.
Aravalli hills, 7.
Arms of Nāgas, 46 ff.
Aryan type, the, 33.
Ashes, footprints in, 239.
Athletic games, 191.
Australian race, connection with India, 26.

BACHELORS' Hall, the, 44, 77.
Bāgh Deo, worship of, 243.
Baghaut, the, 231.
Baiga, the, 210.
—— tribe, 73.
Baiswār tribe, 21.
Baloch tribe, 13, 58 f.
Balti tribe, 52.
Baluchistan, 6, 34.
Banjāra tribe, 117.
Bansapti Ma, worship of, 118, 231.
Bānsphor caste, 103.
Banya caste, 111.
Barhāi, the, 134.
Barham, the, 241.
Barring the ghost, 216.
Basketry, 165.
Bāwaria tribe, 141 f.
Bāzigar caste, 144.
Beena marriage, 209.
Bengali, the, 32.
Beshara Fakīrs, 124.
Bhangi caste, 121.
Bhar tribe, 117.
Bhāt caste, 107.
Bhātu caste, 142.
Bhīl tribe, 25, 66 ff.; magic, 249, 254.
Bhopa, the, 254.
Bhotiya tribe, 12, 49.
Bhuinhār caste, 108.
Bhūt, the, 239.
Birhor tribe, 81.
Birth rites, 194 ff.
Blindman's Buff, 190.
Blood Covenant, the, 208.
Boomerang, the, 26.
Boys' occupations, 180.
Brahma Rākshasa, the, 241.
Brahmans, 94 ff.; priests, 245; of Kashmir, 20.
Brahmaputra river, 3.
Brahui tribe, 27.
Brick-making, 135.
Bronze Age, the, 18.
Burial, 215.

CALICO printing, 138.

Capture marriage, 208.
Carpenters, 134.
Caste, conditions and origin of, 85; democratic, 178.
Caves, 17.
Chamār caste, 122, 196.
Champa tribe, 52.
Chāngar caste, 140.
Chaubē Brahmans, 99.
Children, burial of, 202; life of, 173 ff.; precocity of 174 f.
Chirath tribe, 55.
Churel, the, 231.
Circle charmed, 259.
Circumcision, 204.
Confarreatio, 200, 204.
Cooking, 170.
Copper Age, the, 18.
Cord, the sacred, 201.
Corpse, use of, in Black Magic, 256 f.
Couvade, the, 197.
Cow, sanctity of, 242.
Cremation, 102.
Cricket, 192.
Criminal Tribes, 139.

DACCA muslins, 166.
Dafla tribe, 37.
Dain, the, 262.
Daitya, the, 238.
Dāman-i-Koh, 80.
Dancing, 187.
Dard tribe, 51.
Darzi, the, 138.
Dastūr, 176.
Death Rites, 215 ff.
Deltas, the, 8.
Deo, the, 238.
Devi, worship of, 234.
Devil-dancing, 260.
Dhānuk caste, 120.
Dharkār caste, 103.
Dhobi, the, 120, 139.
Disease caused and removed by Magic, 252.
Doāb, the, 10.
Dom tribe, 13, 101, 217.
Dom Crow game, 189.
Dom Mirāsi, the, 105.
Dosādh tribe, 120.
Dravidian problem, 28; type, 20 ff.
Drugs, collection of, 165.
Dūm Mirāsi, 105.
—— tribe, 53.
Dyeing, 138; women's work in, 168.

EARTH-worship, 232.
Eclipse taboo, 203, 227.
Etiquette, 177.
Evil Eye, protection against, 196.
Exogamy, 206 f.

FAKĪRS, 122 ff.; nudity of, 250.
Farm-work done by women, 168 f.
Fire-walking, 69.
Flour-grinding, 169.
Food, provision and preparation of, 162.
—— and drink, rules regarding, 112.
Footmarks, Magic through, 252.
Fuel-making, 171.

GADIYA Lohārs, 133.
Gagra tribe, 140.
Ganges river, 3; sanctity of, 227.
Gayāl, the, 240.
Gayawāla Brahmans, 99.
Genna taboo, 45.
Ghilzai tribe, 59.
Ghisāra caste, 133.
Gipsy tribes, 120 f., 144.
Girls' games, 192; occupations of, 180, 183.
Gond tribe, 21, 70 ff.; tiger-worship among, 243.
Gotra, the, 207.
Grāma Devata, the, 235.
Gūjar tribe, 114 f., 22.

Gulgulia tribe, 121.
Gurkhas, the, 57.

HABURA tribe, 142.
Hair in Magic, 249 f.
Hārni caste, 140.
Head-hunting, 41 ff.
Himālaya range, 4.
Hindostan, 1.
Hinduism, 223; forest tribes converted to, 75 f.
Home life, 152 ff.
Horoscope, the, 207.
Hunting, woman's share in, 162.
Husbandry, 156 ff.
Hypergamy, 89.

IDOLATRY, 98.
Images, Magic by means of, 248 f.
Imaginativeness of the peasant, 182.
Indo-Aryan type, 20.
Indus river, 3.
Industries, village, 129 ff.
Initiation rites, 200.
Irrigation, 10.

JAT tribe, 92 ff., 112.
Jhabel tribe, 140.
Juang tribe, 12, 77.
Jungle goddesses, 231.

KĀFIRS, 62.
Kaimūr hills, 7.
Kāli, worship of, 234.
Kalwār caste, 119.
Kanet tribe, 55.
Kangra valley, 53.
Kanjar tribe, 145.
Kashmir, 50.
Kayasth caste, 110.
Kāzi, the, 213.
Kehal tribe, 140.
Khasa tribe, 56.
Khatīk caste, 120.
Khatri caste, 109.
Khel or sept, 39.
Kol tribe, 21, 78, 119.
Kolarians, 27.
Kolhāti caste, 144.
Koli tribe, 65.
Kori caste, 120.
Korwa tribe, 245.
Kulin Brahmans, 97.
Kulu valley, 53.
—— rice planting in, 169.
Kumhār caste, 135.
Kunbi, Kurmi caste, 116.

LADAKHI tribe, 52.
Leap-frog, 190.
Lepcha tribe, 23.
Limbu tribe, 23.
Lohār caste, 132.
Loom, the, 137.

MAGHAIYA Doms, 101.
Magic, 246 ff.
—— black, 248.
—— contagious, 248.
—— homœopathic, 248.
—— imitative, 248.
—— in marriage rites, 193.
Mahabrahman caste, 100.
Mahājan caste, 111.
Mahanadi river, 1.
Majhwār tribe, 209 f.
—— marriage rites, 209 f.
Mal, Malē tribe, 22 f., 80.
Māli, the, 116.
Mana, 246.
Manasa, worship of, 243.
Mānjhi tribe, 21.
Mantra, the, 247.
Mari Māta, worship of, 234.
Marriage arrangements, 161.
—— infant, 183.
—— rites, 206 ff.
Mārwāri Banya caste, 111.
Meo tribe, 143.
Metal workers, 131 f.

Metempsychosis, 201.
Mīna tribe, 140, 143.
Miri tribe, 37.
Mohammedans, birth rites, 203.
—— death rites, 219 f.
—— marriage rites, 212.
—— social grouping of, 124 f.
Mohwa, the, 162.
Mongoloid type, the, 23 f., 31.
Moon-worship, 226.
Mosque, the village, 154.
Mother-in-law, the, 186.
Mountain-worship, 229.
Mourning, Hindu, 217.
—— Mohammedan, 221.
Munda tribe, 78.
Munkar, 220.

NĀGA tribe of Assam, 37 ff.
—— death rites, 215.
—— exorcism, 261.
—— tribe in the west, 55.
Nakīr, 220.
Name-giving, 199, 204.
Nat tribe, 144.
Nature, knowledge of, 181.
—— spirits, 226.
Nerbudda river, 1.
Newār tribe, 57.
Nudity in magic, 249 f.

OD tribe, 140.
Opium collecting, 171.
Oraon tribe, 76.
—— magic, 251.

PAHARIA tribe, 79.
Pakhiwāra tribe, 140.
Pandit, the, 95.
Pāsi caste, 120.
Pathān tribe, 60 ff.
—— problem of, 5.
Pilgrims, 98 f.
Pisācha, the, 239.
Pitri, the, 219.
Plains, the, 11.
Planets, the, 227.
Plants, knowledge of, 182.
Polyandry, 49, 207.
Pottery, 135.
—— woman's work in, 166.
Prisoners' Base, 188 f.
Proverbs, 182.
Prayāgwāl Brahmans, 99.
Purchase marriage, 208.
Purohit, the, 95.

RAINFALL, 9 f., 11.
Rain-making, 250.
Rāji tribe, 104, 119.
Rajmahāl hills, 7.
Rajputs, 88 ff.
—— in the hills, 53.
Rakshasa, the, 237.
Rathi tribe, 55.
Rebirth, doctrine of, 201.
Rest-houses, 155.
Rice husking, 169.
—— transplanting, 169.
River-worship, 227 f.
Rope-making, 166.

SAFED Koh range, 1.
Salīm Chishti, the saint, 203.
Sānsi tribe, 140.
Santāl tribe, 81 ff., 162, 207, 253.
Seclusion of mother and child, 198.
Sema tribe, 41.
Shaman, Shamanism, 68, 259.
Shashthi, worship of, 198.
Sikhs, 93.
Sītala, worship of, 234.
Snake-worship, 242 f.
Sonār caste, 131.
Soul, its state after death, 218.
Spells, 254 f.
Spinning, 166.
Srāddha, the, 218 f.
Stone implements, 16.
Sulaimān range, 1.

Sun-worship, 226.
Sweeper castes, 121

TABOO, 164, 194 f., 216.
Taga caste, 109.
Tailoring, 138.
Tarkhān, the, 134.
Tartan of Nāgas, 48.
Tattooing, 145, 165.
Teli caste, 119.
Temple priests, 98.
Terai, the, 9.
Thāru tribe, 118.
Thori caste, 140.
Tiger, spells to repell, 256.
—— worship, 242.
Tip-cat, 188.
Totemism in marriage, 206.
—— in religion, 244.
Trees, sacred, 230.
Tribe, the, 36 f.
Tusser silk, 164.

UTTARA KURUS, the, 50.

VAGRANT tribes, 139.
Vaishnava Fakīrs, 123.
Village, the, 126 ff.
—— Aryan and Dravidian, 31.
—— gods, 235.
—— of the Nāgas, 39.
—— servants, 129.
Vindhyan hills, 7.

WASHERMAN, the, 139.
Weaving, 136.
Wells and tanks, 155 f.
—— sacred, 228.
Widow marriage, 209.
Witch, the, 262.
Women, occupations of, 161.
—— social life of, 160 ff.

NORTHERN INDIA
AFGHANISTAN
BALUCHISTAN
KASHMIR
CHINESE EMPIRE
PUNJAB
RAJPUTANA
SIND
BOMBAY PRESIDENCY
NORTH-WEST PROVS AND OUDH
CENTRAL INDIAN AGENCY
CENTRAL PROVINCES
NEPAL
BHUTAN
BENGAL
ASSAM
BURMAH
ARABIAN SEA
BAY OF BENGAL
Kabul
Quetta
Srinagar
Rawalpindi
Jehlam
Lahore
Amritsar
Multan
Simla
Ambala
Kumaun
Garhwal
Delhi
Naini Tal
Bahawalpur
Bikaner
Jaisalmir
Marwar
Jodhpur
Ajmir
Jaipur
Agra
Lucknow
Gwalior
Jhansi
Cawnpur
Allahabad
Ganges
Benares
Patna
Bundelkhand
Malwa
Bhopal
Narbada
Gujarat
Kathiawar
Karachi
Shikarpur
Udaipur
Mewar
Amarkantak
Chutia Nagpur
R. Mahanadi
Orissa
Juggernauth
Bardwan
Calcutta
Darjiling
Kuch Behar
Bhagalpur
Everest
Kanchanjanga
Brahmaputra
Naga Hills
Khasi Hills
Hill Tipperah
Dacca